AF278840

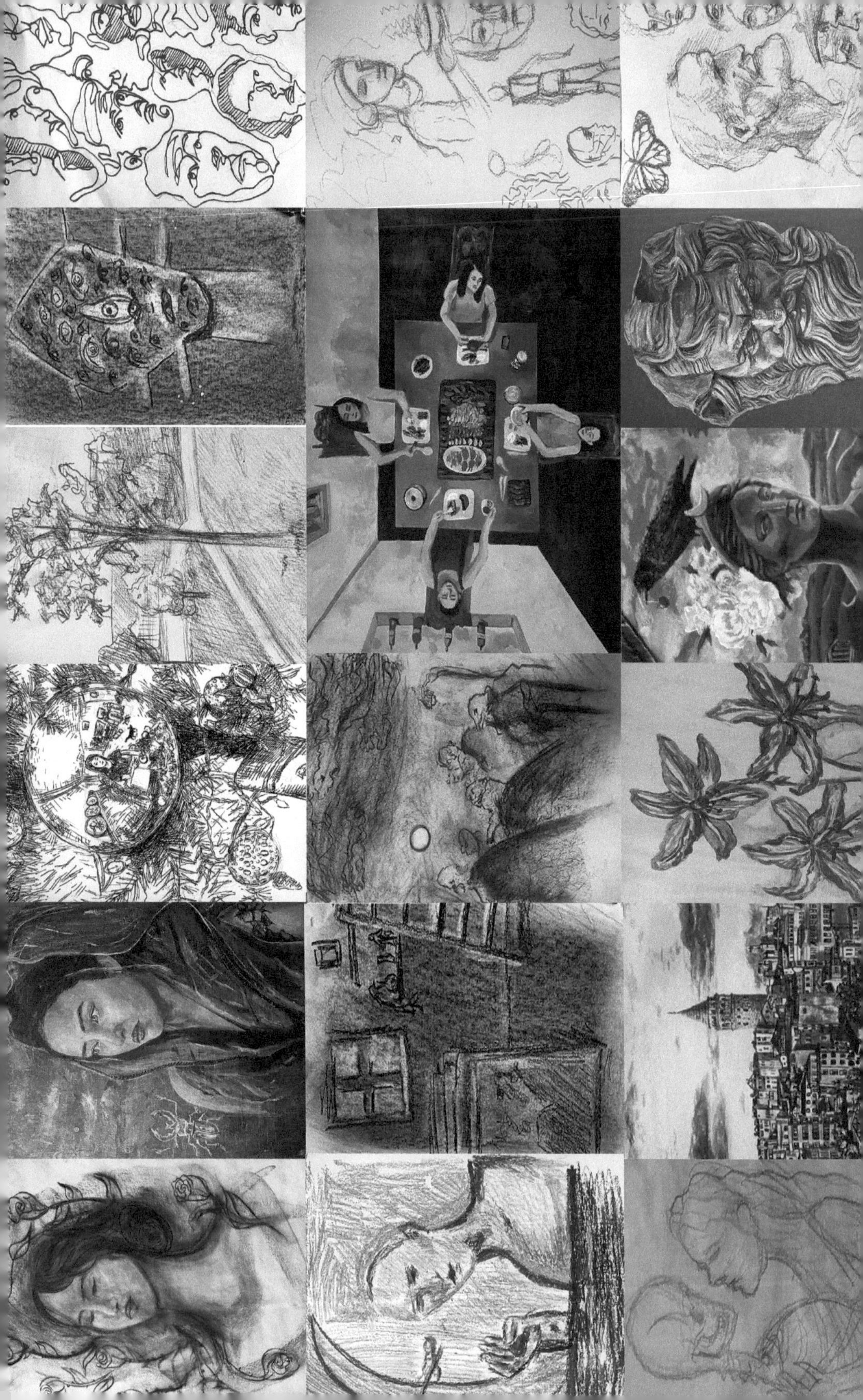

INTERCONNECTEDNESS

A Collection of Poetry and Art

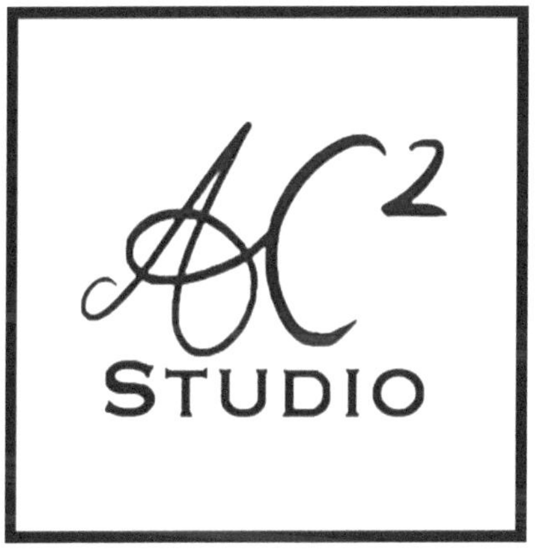

By Angelica Comia Candido

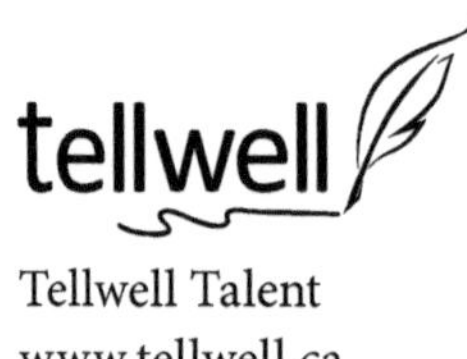

Tellwell Talent
www.tellwell.ca

ISBN
978-1-0690191-0-3 (Paperback)
978-1-0690191-1-0 (eBook)

ACKNOWLEDGEMENTS

I am deeply grateful to my family—Eric, Bernadette, Pauline, and Paul Candido—for being the backbone of support in all my creative endeavors. A heartfelt thank you to my friends for their patience and belief in me, especially Cynthia and Megan, whose encouragement inspired me to publish this book. Lastly, my sincere thanks to all my readers and followers. Your interest and support mean the world to me and make this journey truly worthwhile.

ABOUT THE AUTHOR

Storytime: Angelica Candido

From a young age, I was drawn to exploring my creative nature and finding inspiration in everything around me. Born in Manila, Philippines, and raised in Brampton, Canada, with a year spent abroad in Istanbul, Turkey, my journey has been shaped by diverse cultural experiences. I love experimenting with various artistic mediums, including acrylic paint, gouache, digital art, oil paints, and pencil. Beyond art, I enjoy exercising, learning about business and entrepreneurship, practicing meditation and mindfulness, spending time with loved ones, reading, traveling, journalling, and teaching art. In 2020, I began writing poetry to delve deeper into my emotions, which have now been compiled in this book.

Interconnectedness – A Collection of Poetry and Art explores personal experiences from 2020 to 2024, aiming to evoke a sense of calm in readers.

Painting is silent poetry.
Without words,
it engraves meaning
to the heart.

Colors evoke emotion,
lines drift in space.
Don't let this mystery
of creation depart.

TABLE OF CONTENTS

PART I

THE PAST

There are moments in one's life that become a turning point. A peek that causes one to change, to contemplate, and to be reborn. For me, that was when my brother passed away on July 5th, 2020, due to a sudden accident. Around this time, my long-term relationship finished and one of my cats passed away. This was during the pandemic and lockdown, so one can only imagine how much an overthinker can spiral. It put me into an existential loophole, questioning life every day, which was no way to live. Ironically, this is what drove me to liberate myself. During this time of dread, I turned to art to express these emotions or to escape the reality that haunted me. I was reborn, healed, free from the chains that tried to hold me back, and ultimately, free from myself and the negative outlook I had on life. Both these negative and positive polarities are expressed in this book that travels from past to present. Aside from expressing my emotions with my art, I use it as an instrument to convey my dreams, research, and symbolism which are explained in the subsequent pages. The title "Interconnectedness" demonstrates that we are all inextricably connected to one another, animals, stars, and land, while experiencing this moment in time.

Before realizing this point, I had to go through the hurt, the pain, the stormy nights before the calm day.

Glimpses of treasure found in your eyes.
Carried by the waves of the past.
The calm serenity or the mountain peak of happiness
that we once shared.

We forget to live in that moment,
to treasure it as if it won't one day
become another distant memory.
To treasure the people we surround ourselves with.

Remember what it was like to love.
Time passes by and in it, fills with worry,
insecurity, toxicity, anger, lust —
leaving no room for love.

Sometimes it's nice to look back,
to be in that state of mind,
being with eternity.
Remember to be conscious.

Be present with each breath
before we get older,
and this impression left on the heart
begins to fade away.

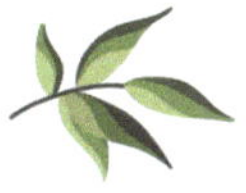

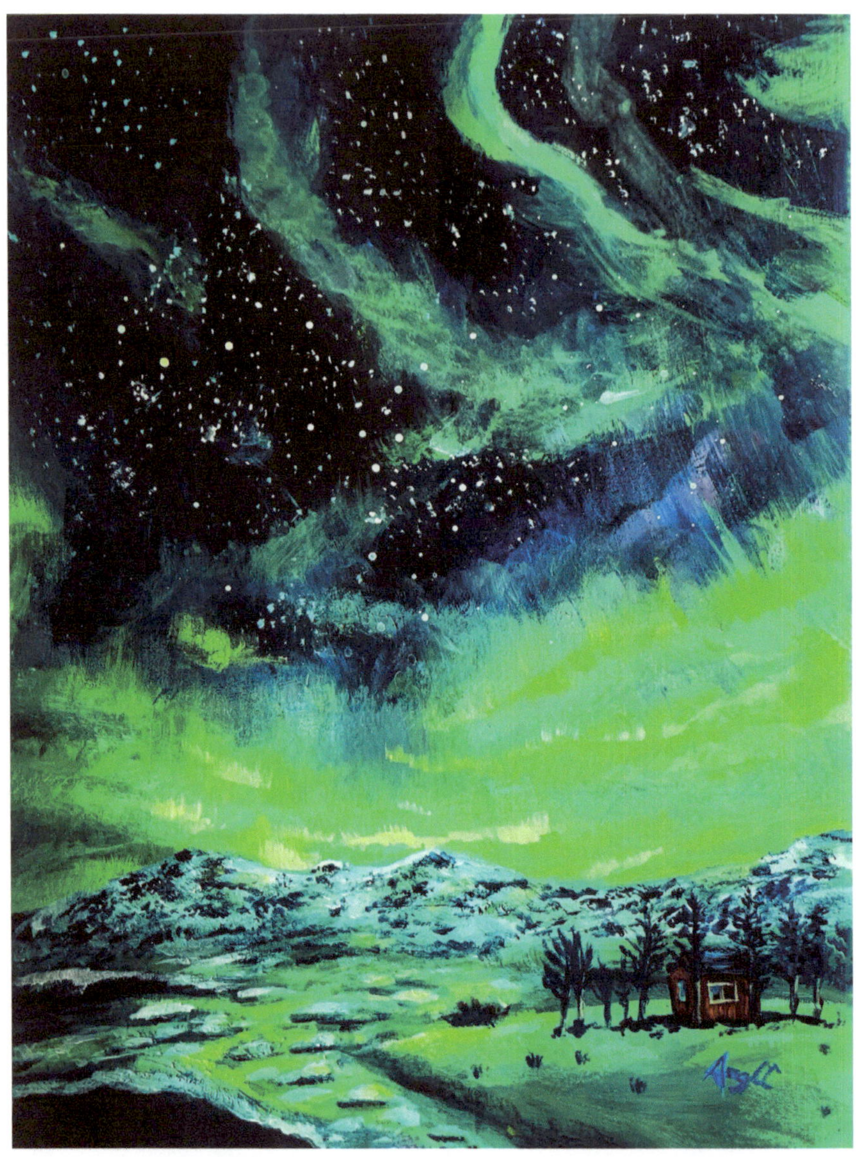

Northern Lights. Acrylic on mixed media paper. 8"x11"in, 2021.

Weak bricks lay in the foundation of a new home.
It collapses once the roof is made.
Then you ask me why we didn't work out.
I'll point to the rickety bricks and tell you this:

There is no room for support,
nor foundation strong enough to bolster up your magnitude —
a place wide enough for your significance,
or a floor plan to get there.

We begin to build anyway out of pure
curiosity and love for building.
Hammering the nails and bolts,
we open the door to the new home.

It was a safe space for centuries to come.
Once we enter inside,
bricks break
and crushes everything we built.

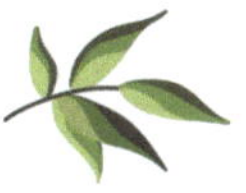

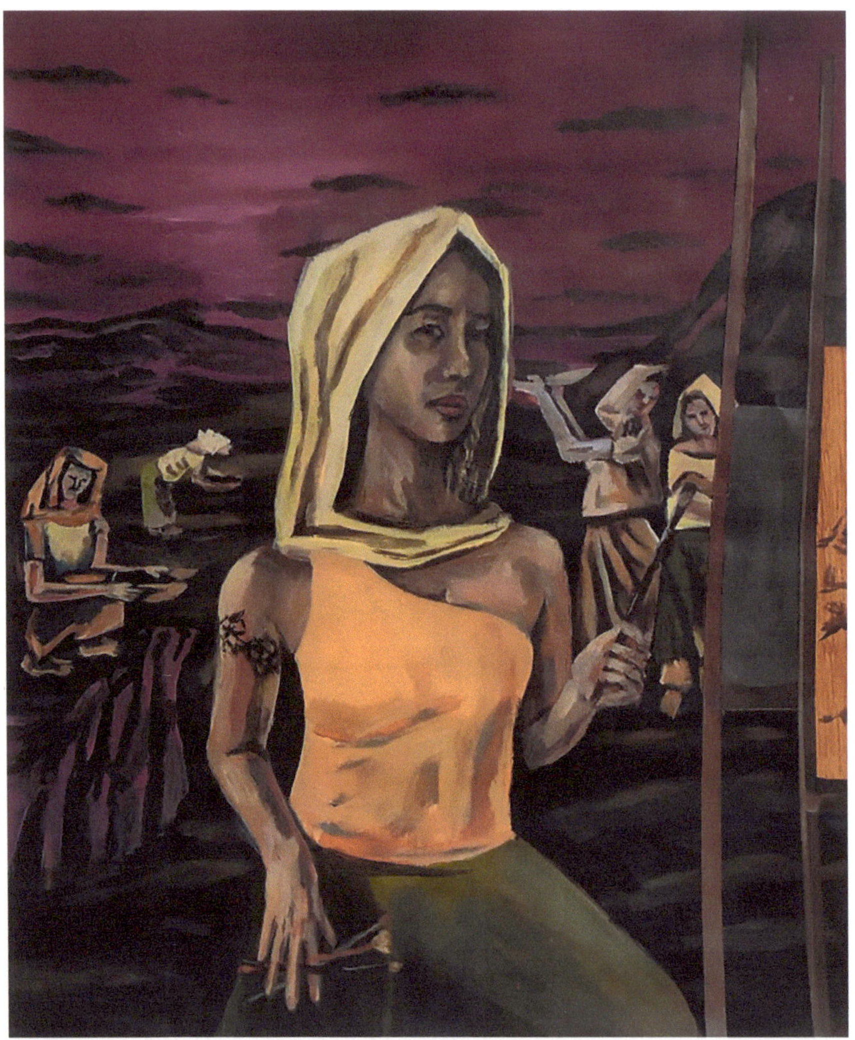

Self-Portrait in Great-Grandma's painting. Acrylic on paper, 12"x15"in, 2022.

Where do souls go when they die?
Does it perish away or float
through the endless sky?

Maybe it rests next to the beloved's throne.
Or in the meadows green and lush,
far away from home.

I've thought about death a lot this past year.
Only to realize that to live
and to die is just as near.

The aftermath I question
longing for the answer,
but that's the mystery.
Looking for reasons legends live on
all throughout history.

A beginning to the end of the
harmonious lived story.

Maybe it's not such a bad thing
to be reminded of what it's like
to feel love.

Even though it's in the past,
I shouldn't ridicule
the mornings because you
were in my dreams.

Perhaps I need to feel it once more.
Cherish the nostalgic memories
and be happy in the present.
Knowing that love doesn't stop.

It grows within you,
even in sleep.

I was aware of my flaws,
but I was incapable of fixing them.

Beyond these intense emotions,
there is an elixir that nourishes —
blinded by false pretenses.

I dwelled in the memories like the
moon's reflection on the riverbed.
Voices clamoring now
though it was just in my head.

No place was safe to hide
it was the station with the same old song.
Till one day I realized the remedy
was the love inside me all along.

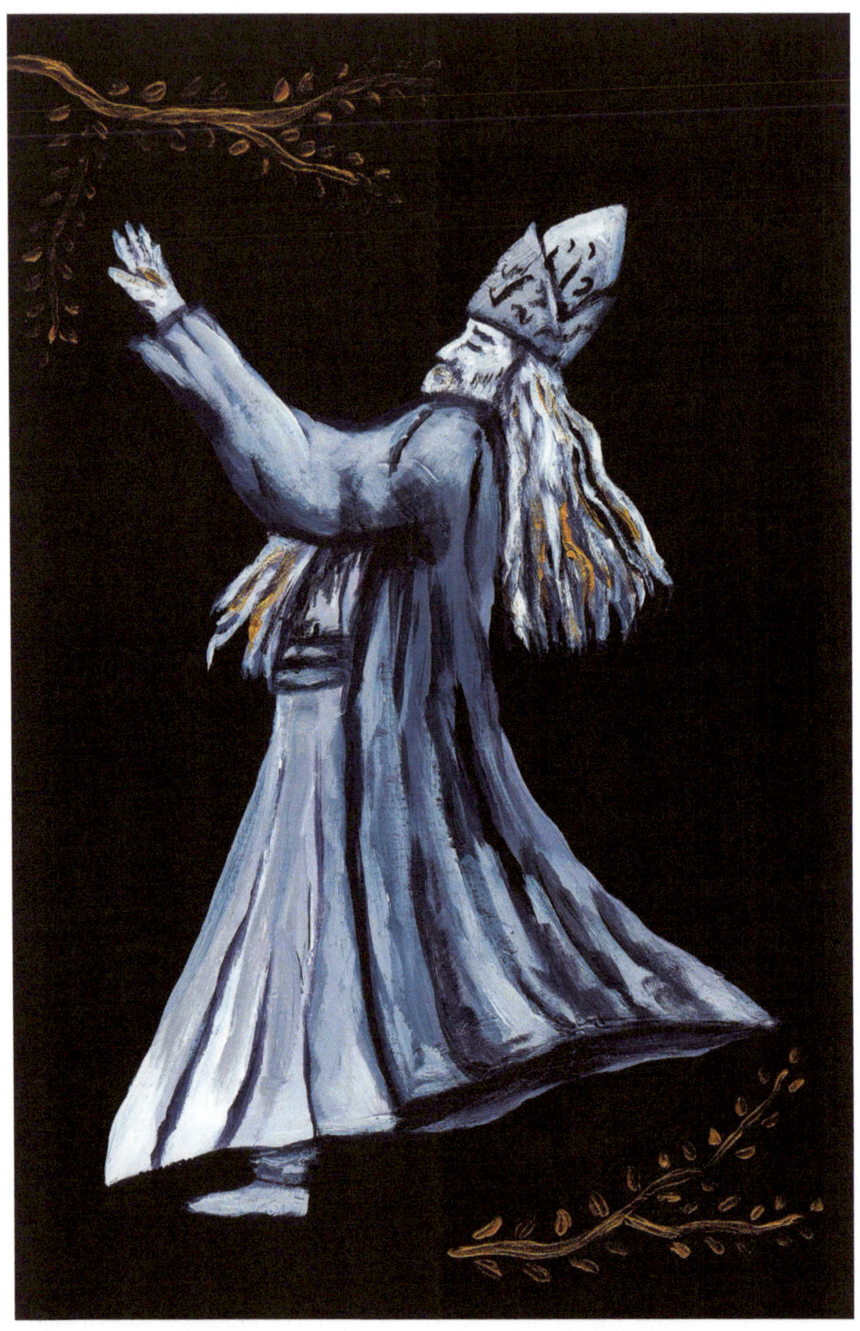

Whirling Dervish. Acrylic on paper, 6"x8"in, 2021.

Do I fill the giant void
that you left in my heart
with meaningless desires?

I don't know who you are
or where I'm going.

I'm told to go where the heart yearns
without a roadmap or route,
expecting light will shine through.

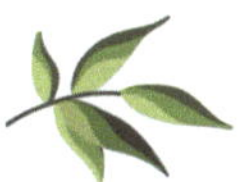

I wish I told you how nice you looked
under the stars and moon shine.
How your face glowed throughout the sky
as you put your lips on mine.

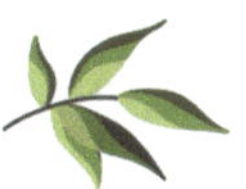

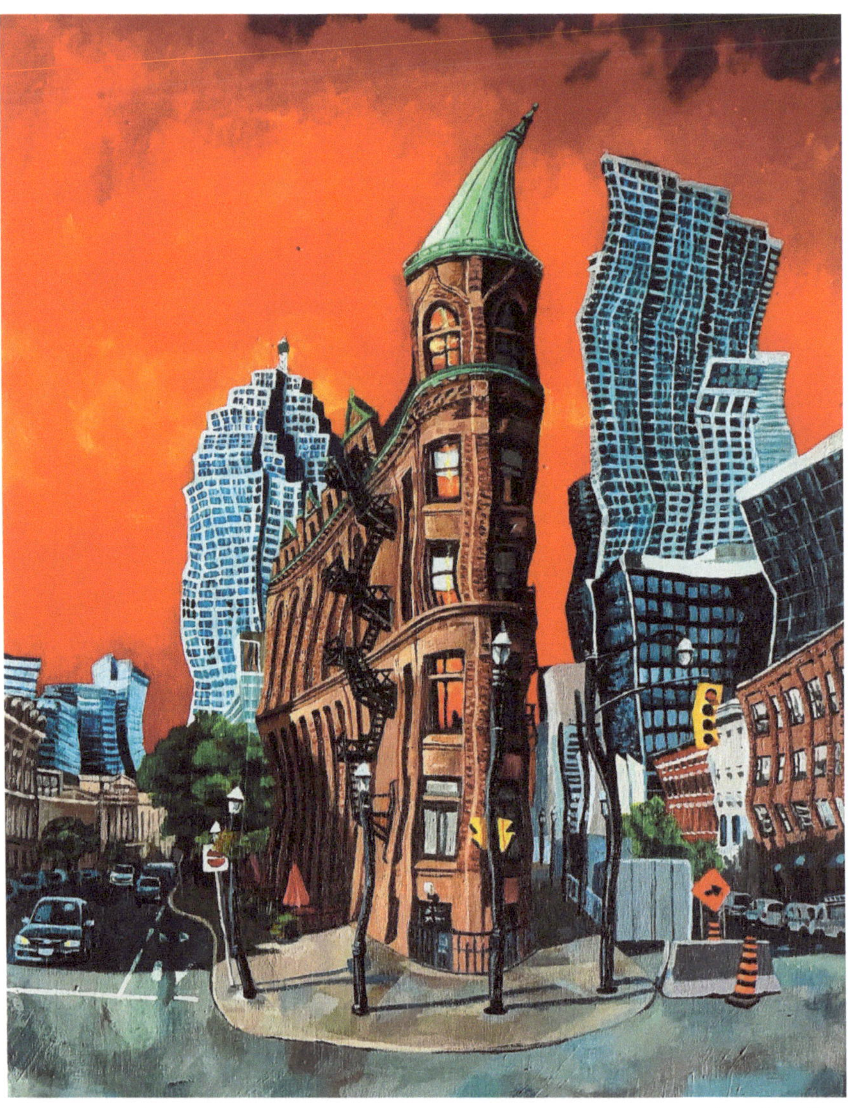

Beginning of Distortion, acrylic on premium artist canvas panel, 18"x24"in, 2020. This scene takes place in The Gooderham Building, Toronto. The distortion represents the year 2020, taking unexpected turns from the coronavirus, political upheavals, and natural disasters. The intensity of the red is used to amplify an ominous feeling we mostly face during times of uncertainty

Sometimes I forget our words and phrases,
what we did or memories we shared.
Though there wasn't a time I could forget
the infinite love you made me feel.

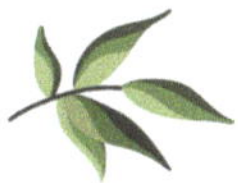

I can create more beautiful things.
How freeing is it to constantly create?
To have the ability to make something your own.

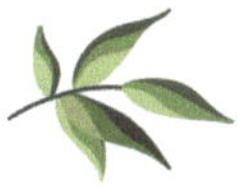

I have compiled hundreds of sketches,
paintings, and words written on paper.
Yet with all the piles of art, craft, and wordy affirmations,
nothing compares to seeing you once again.

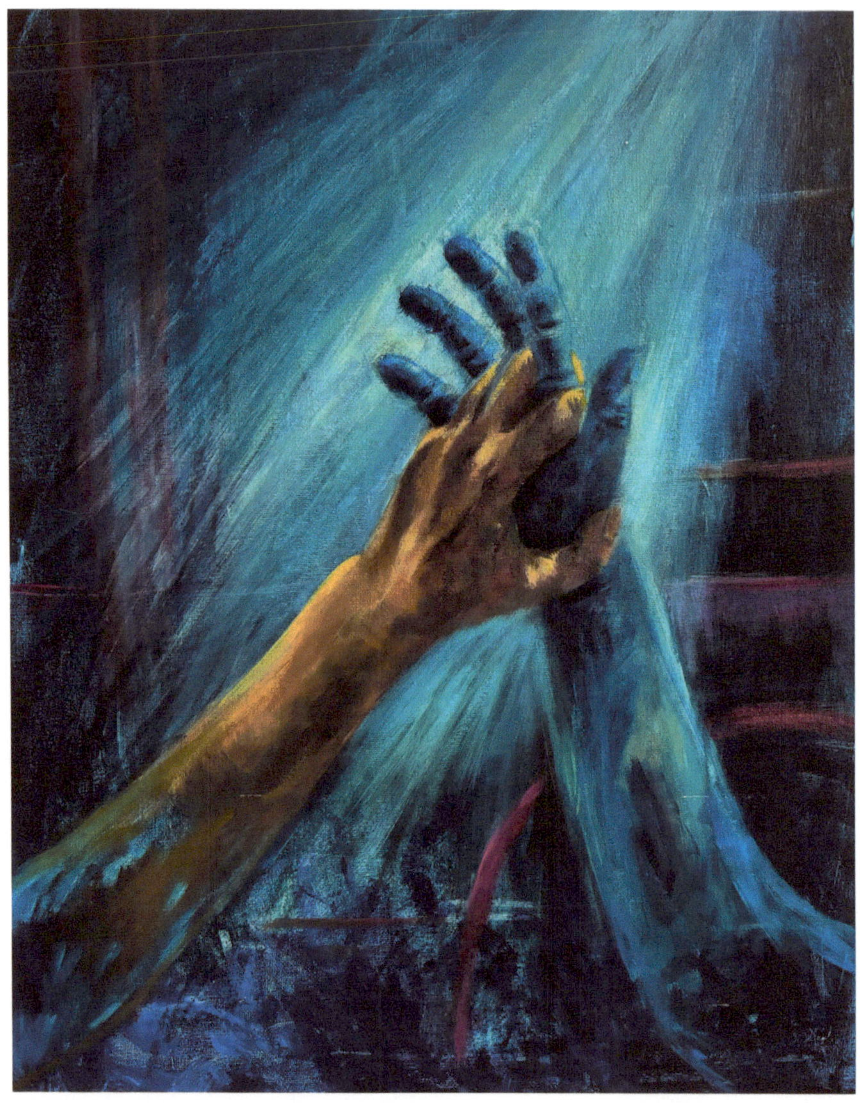

Longing, mixed media on canvas, 18"x16", 2024. This painting captures a dream I had of my brother. He was in my sister's room, and I questioned whether he was truly gone. Telepathically, he answered, "Yes, what do you want to know?" I replied, "I just want to hold your hand."

Gone but not for long

If there comes a time
when I forget your smile,
I'll need to ground myself again
to remember what makes life worthwhile.

If there comes a time
that memories no longer serve me,
bring me close to the earth once more
to know how things should be.

If the unknown is where you stand
without any left-over trace,
I'll have the satisfaction of knowing
that your memory is left with grace.

If I let you into
the deepest parts of me,
promise that you won't
wither and run free.

Hold pieces of my heart
they're now yours to take.
Find me again across infinity
for old times' sake.

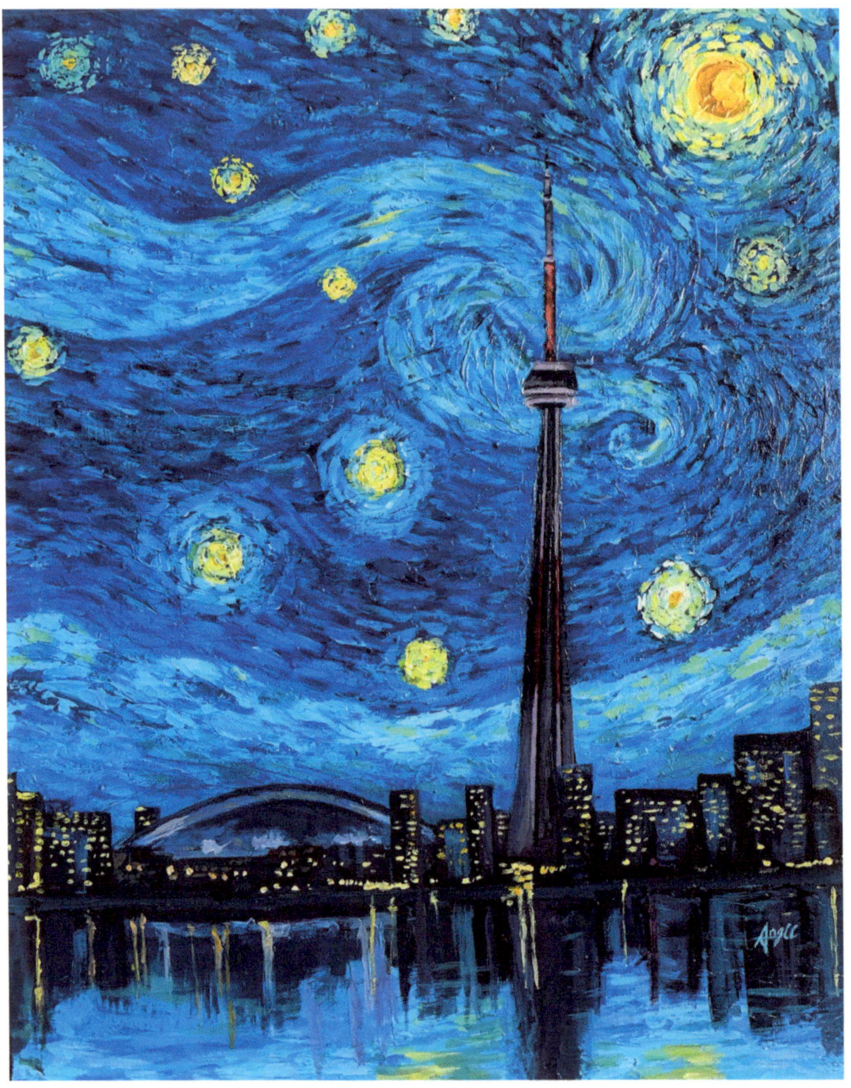

Starry Toronto Night. Mixed media on canvas, 20"x14"in, 2020.

Relationships are like a game of chess,
the queen moves in the direction of the king,
guarded by the rook and knight —
more walls than the eye can see.

There's no checkmate here,
not even the intention of coming near.
Playing the fool's game, we become cautious,
hesitating on the next move.

Unwanted actions from lack of precaution,
the goal is near, yet far away.
Just coming close for intensity
caught in the tension of play.

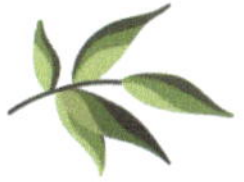

Do ashes fall generously
with lust and desire mingling in the air?
Entwining effortlessly.
Warmth of fire on the skin,
breathing this ecstasy of life.

Fire endlessly burning the substance,
from the tip of your fingertips
slowly slipping into the ashtray.
Back to the separated particles,
where it all began.

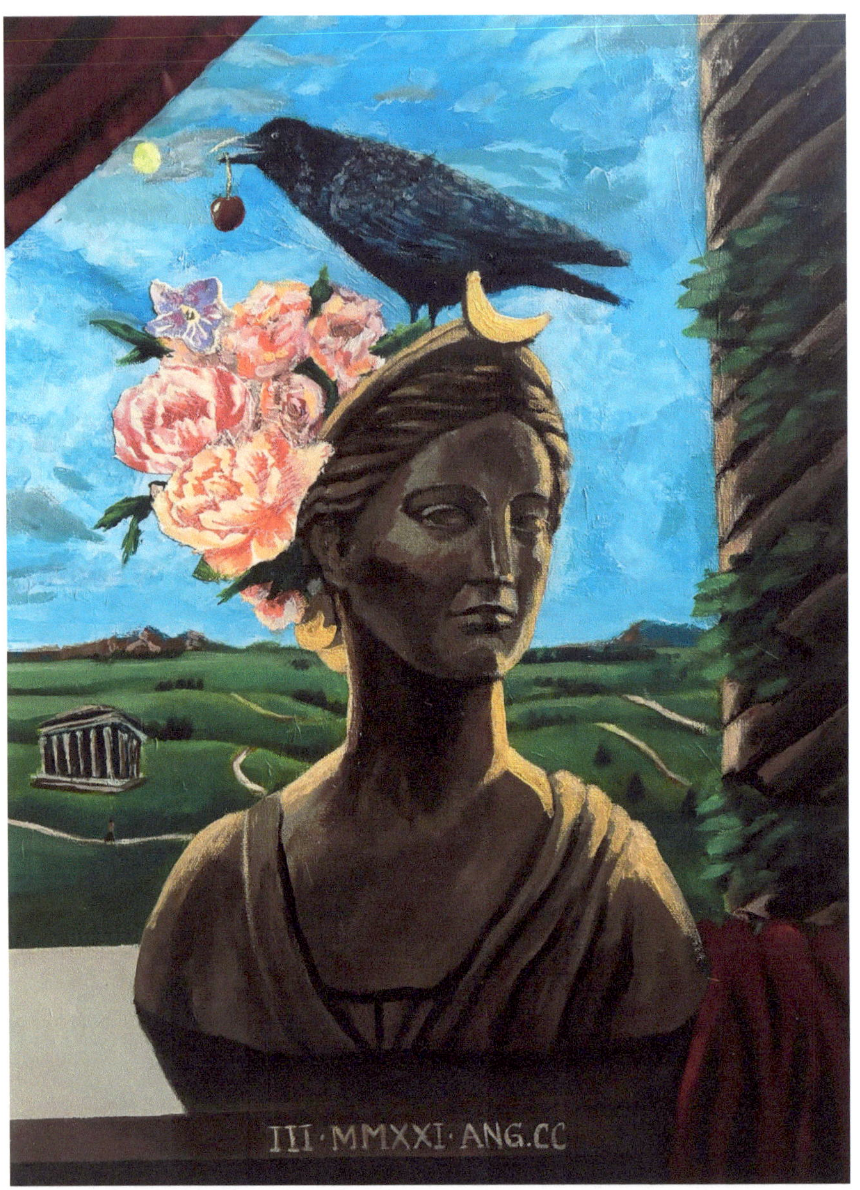

Nike on a Landscape, mixed media on canvas, 24"x18"in, 2021.

There it was, in the palm of my hand,
where I once felt
the touch of a thousand waves at once.
Banishing as fast as it came in.

We mustn't think of this as a loss
but as a new beginning with each day.
It presents opportunities.

Like a bird with a golden egg.
What seemed special and worth hanging on to
is sometimes best left alone.
Who knows?

Maybe the golden egg hatches
and out reveals a rabid offspring.

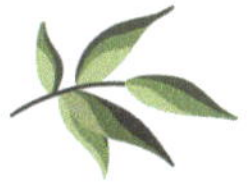

I wanted to forget about
the memories we had.
Move on without any ties,
while venturing off ahead.

But what if I stumble
backward in a trap,
hours of silence to hear
a thunderous clap?

The unexpected comes-
a joy from above.
Lost hope is found here
by those who strive for love.

PART II

SEPARATION. NON-ATTACHMENT.

Separation. Since childhood, whether through death, falling apart in friendships, or relationships, abandonment has always made me uneasy. I carried this fear into my relationships, often replaying scenarios of potential breakups, which likely contributed to their eventual collapse. When my relationship ended, I missed my previous cat who stayed with my former partner. Then one day, I saw an abandoned black cat wandering the forest with an empty cage nearby. She seemed wary and alone. I decided to feed her every morning for two months, naming her Buwan, meaning "Moon" in Tagalog. Though I rarely saw her, her food was always gone the next day. When I did spot her, she was skittish, running away whenever I approached. Eventually, she was caught by a local woman and we took her to a shelter. Within weeks, I was able to bring her home. Since then, Buwan has been a loving companion and muse. She's no longer afraid of people, always kneading on me and accompanying me as I create. Now well-fed and thriving, she is a reminder that healing can come from the most unexpected places.

Non-Attachment. Having lost important people in my life, I've had to embrace the concept of impermanence—learning to let go, pick myself up, and manage my mental health. Growing up, I struggled with depression and insecurities, facing negative experiences repeatedly. Eventually, I found peace in expressing myself through art. I focused on improving my drawing and painting skills to maintain my creative flow, even on days when emotional burdens were prominent. To cope with separation and endings, I practiced non-attachment, striving for inner peace and balance while navigating daily routines.

Moving forward, I now embrace a new perspective, free from limiting beliefs to foster growth, courage, and perseverance. Though this path can be challenging, persistence leads to new opportunities, people, and experiences. For details on my healing process, refer to Part 5: The Healing Journey.

I love you

If I can go back in time
to my younger self at her lowest,
I'd pull her in closely,
embrace her, and say,

"Who you are is worth
all the love you're willing
to give to someone else.

It's you who needs the
love first. You're enough.
You've always been enough.

You're loved in your
darkest days, stronger
than you think in the
loneliest nights. I wish I could tell you
this every single day.

But I'll be here with you.
Always. And if you ever need a reminder,
tune into the beating of your heart."

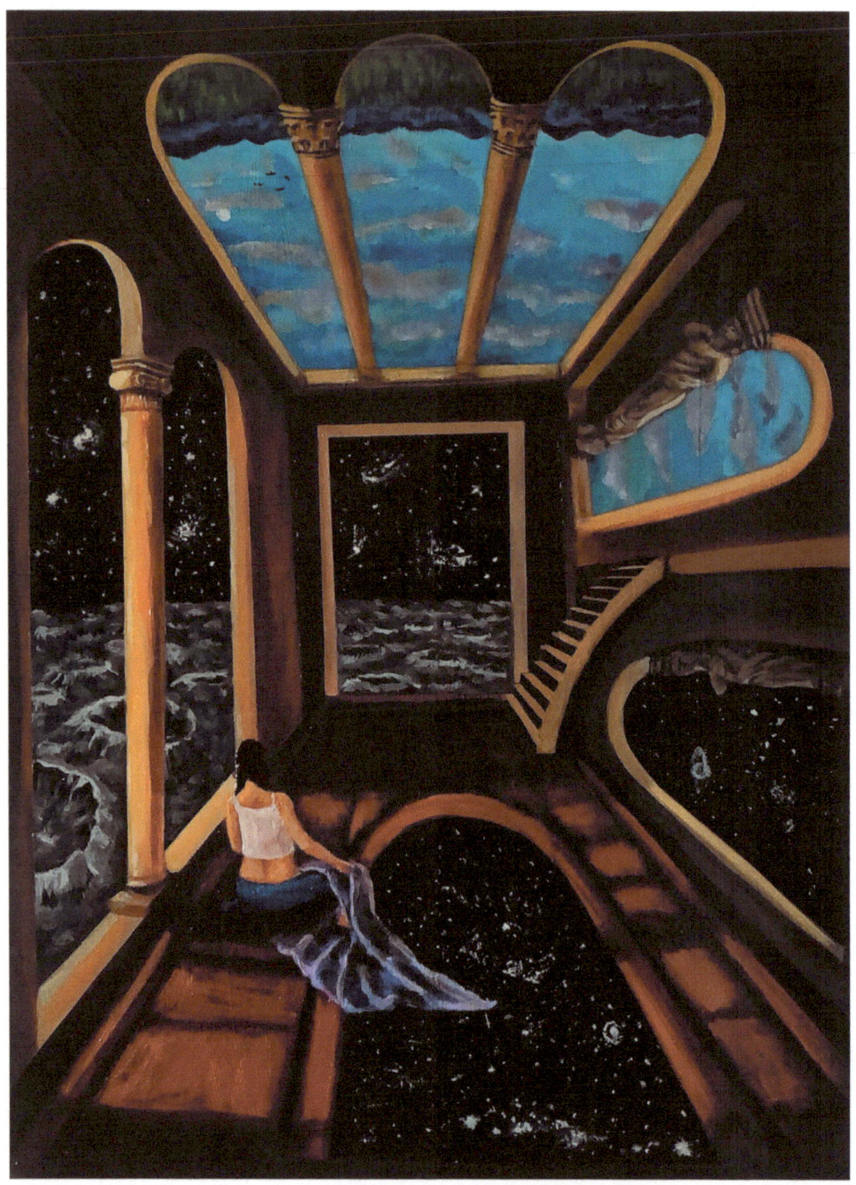

Lost in Dreamland. Acrylic on canvas, 24"x18"in, 2022.

Opening the Grave

It was selfish to let
you walk back into my life -
wounds finally healed
only to be cut open by a knife.

Leaving behind no trace of emotion,
just a blurred face.
Unspoken words, broken feelings,
left untied like a shoelace.

Pulling me back in your arms,
the past and future intertwined,
until only memories remain
from the passion we left behind.

Midnight flashes from
that feeling of comfort is gone.
It's better to keep looking forward
and push to move on.

Past the lonely days and nights,
from the times that felt so blue.
To where the sun rises and falls
until there's no longer a sight of you.

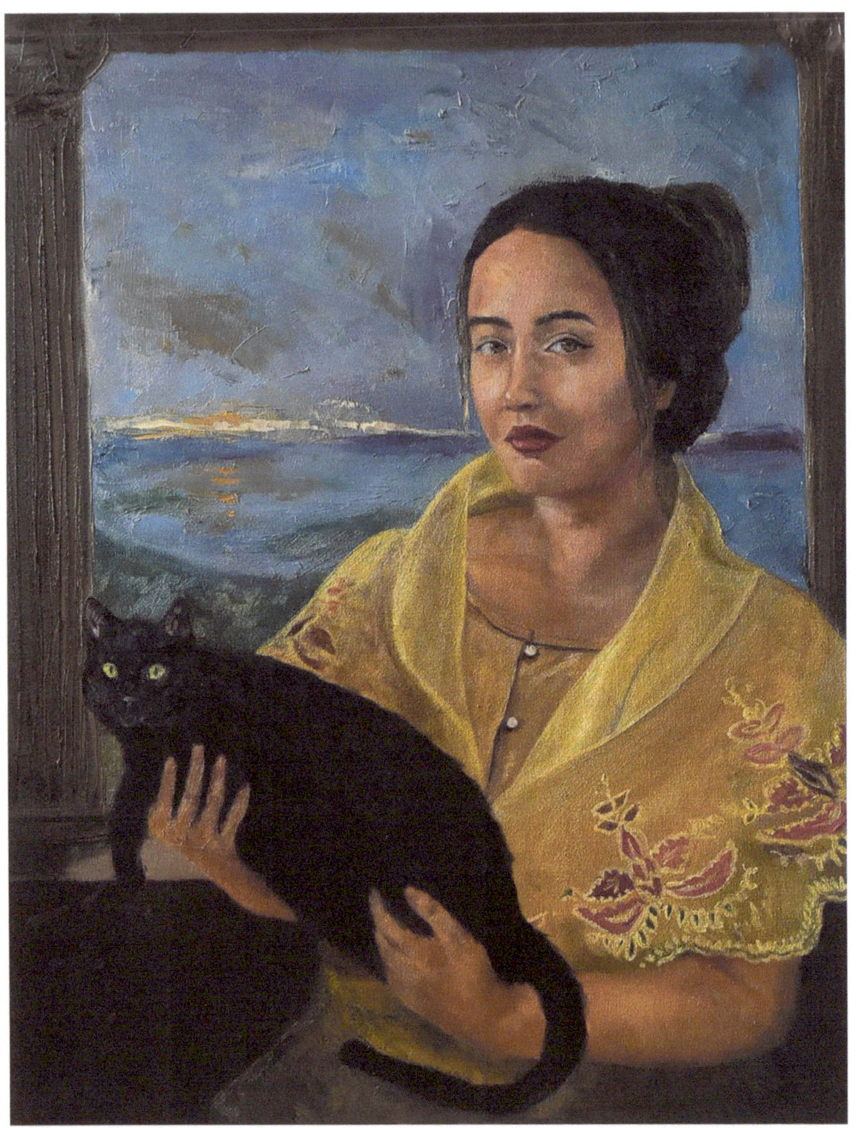

Self-Portrait With my Cat. Oil paint on canvas, 18"x16"in, 2024.

One is made whole when
reunified with her loved one.
Like a loaf of bread in the oven,
rising with excitement when done.

Tell me I'm yours once more,
that this is all you need.
So that we can emerge perfectly
like a sprout from a seed.

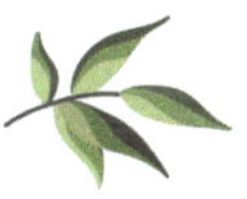

Blooming with new colours and textures,
a spring garden has filled my yard.
There is no picking flowers here,
just the tranquility that I invite you to join.

Out of the barren wasteland where nothing grew
sparked something different and new.
Running through this endless array of fantasies.
You grab my hand and bring me back to reality.

Oh love, there are lessons upon lessons.
I've been running a race in my mind.
Now the door is wide open to explore
leaving the traces of the past behind.

This magic happens to the mature soul —
a kind of purification after initiation.
Togetherness or this loneliness,
I've cried for both and for no reason.

It was clear all along that oil and water don't mix.
Yet we tried, hand in hand, to make it work.
We mixed, boiled, shook it together,
in the end, it remained separated.

Who designed it in such a way that
they can never fully dissolve into one another?
Instead, we move to invisible forces,
encapsulated in a vessel,
dancing separately together.

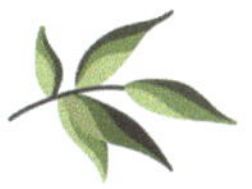

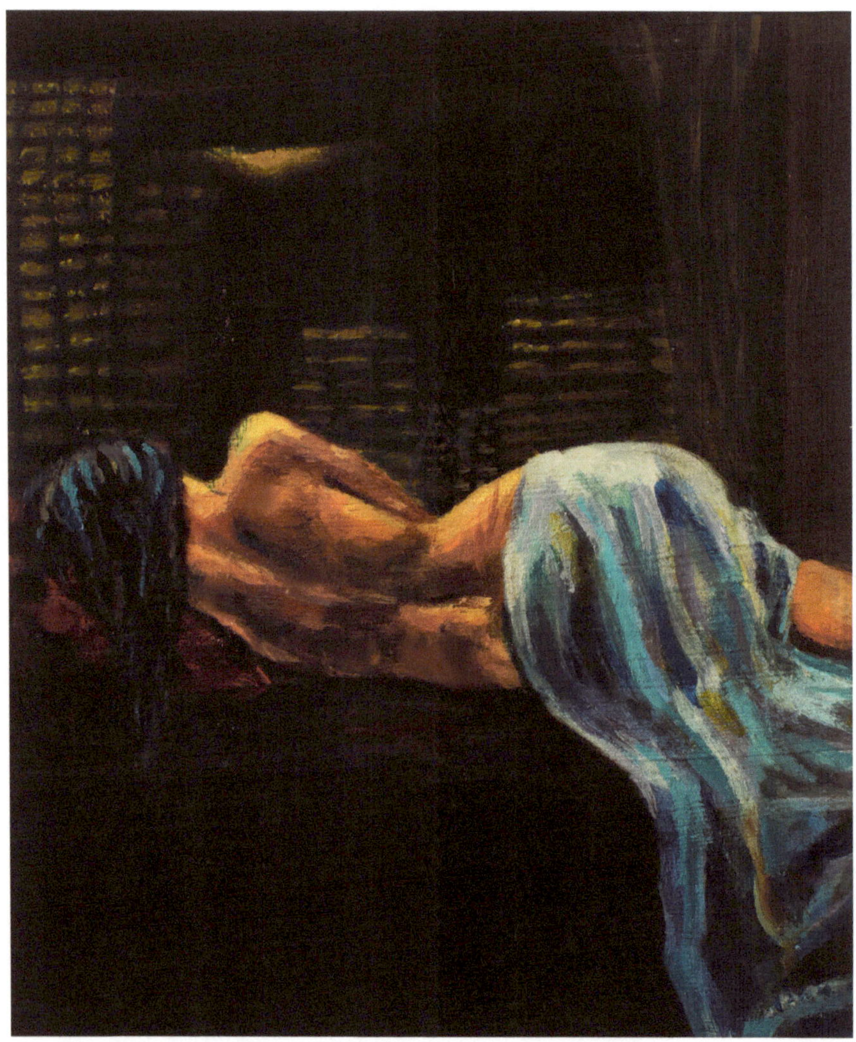

Resting. Acrylic on wood, 6"x8"in, 2021.

Feeling like a slug.
Wrapped in my
blanket for a shell.

Laying on the bed
in the comfort
of my thoughts
is where I dwell.

To be human
and keep pushing
is gone from my needs.

No one to disturb
the peaceful encounter
and where it leads.

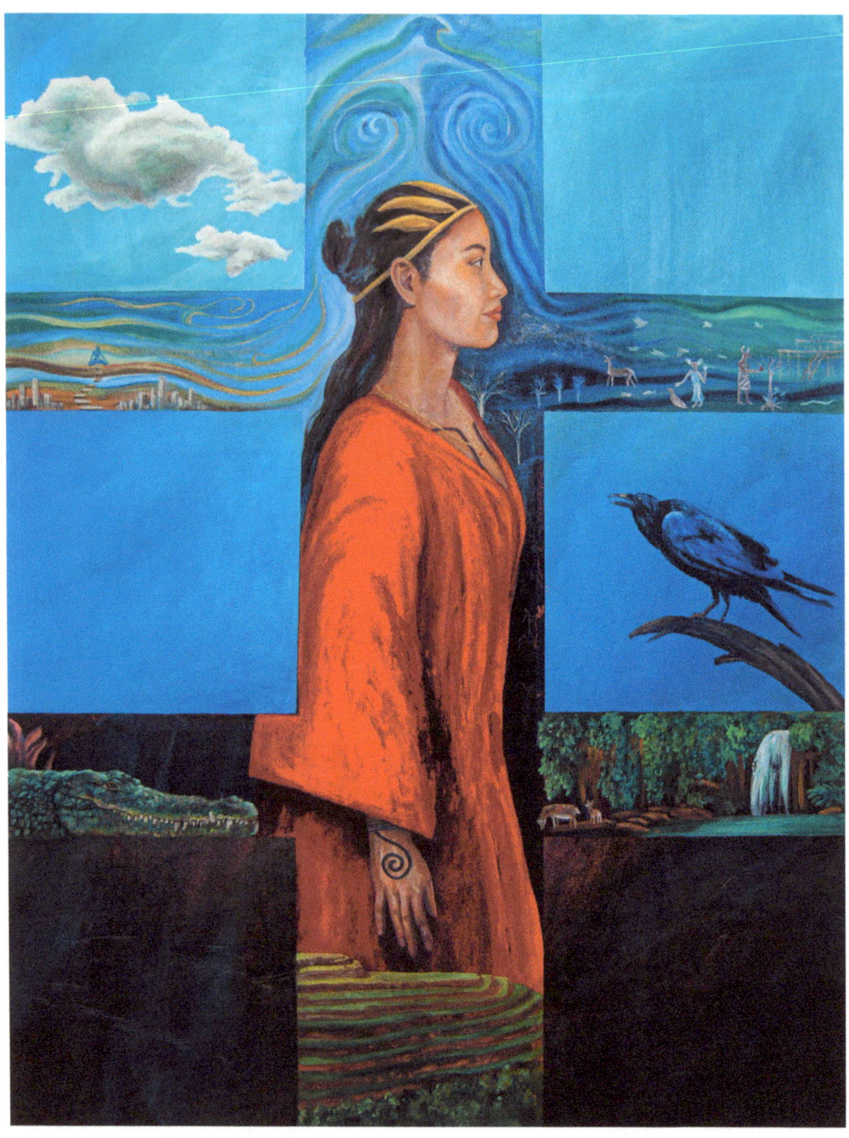

Window to the Soul. Oil paint, acrylic paint, oil pastel, modeling paste on canvas, 52"x65"in, 2023. While exploring my Filipino culture and stories from the past, I wanted to depict an ancestor standing strong in the center with nature surrounding her since the Philippines is known for its stunning landscapes. There's hidden symbolism and inspiration derived from my dreams throughout this painting such as the crocodile, a sacred animal for the ancient Tagalog people as it was believed they carry the soul of a deceased person.

Letting go

When is it the right time
to practice non-attachment?
After every single breath.

The liberating feeling —
realizing that nothing in this world
is ours to begin with.
It all starts and ends the same
in the hands of the creator.

So why do we humans attach ourselves
to emotions, objects, or people?
Let go and surrender
to the divine work of magic unfolding.

Society's expectations —
the only thing permanent
is impermanence.

In one second,
everything can change.
There's no use of clinging
or trying to fight it.

Like each inhale,
waiting for an exhale,
the best thing to do is breathe with it
and trust that it's for the best.

That the world is not
conspiring against you
instead, it's making you learn,
experience, and grow.

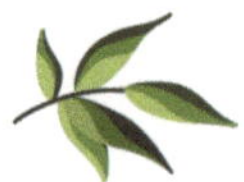

It was the world that convinced me
that I wasn't enough,
that it got through my head
and I believed it myself.

I wonder why trust issues are created,
why I couldn't love fully in relationships —
the comparing, the feeling inadequate,
riddled with insecurity and jealousy.

What I've gone through shows the strength
of a warrior who has fought her battles,
rising to the battlefield to prove her worth,
Standing tall, she declares:
"Enough. It's time I give myself what I deserve."

It's not his fault or hers.
It's my fault for letting it go on
longer than it should have,
only damaging myself in the process.

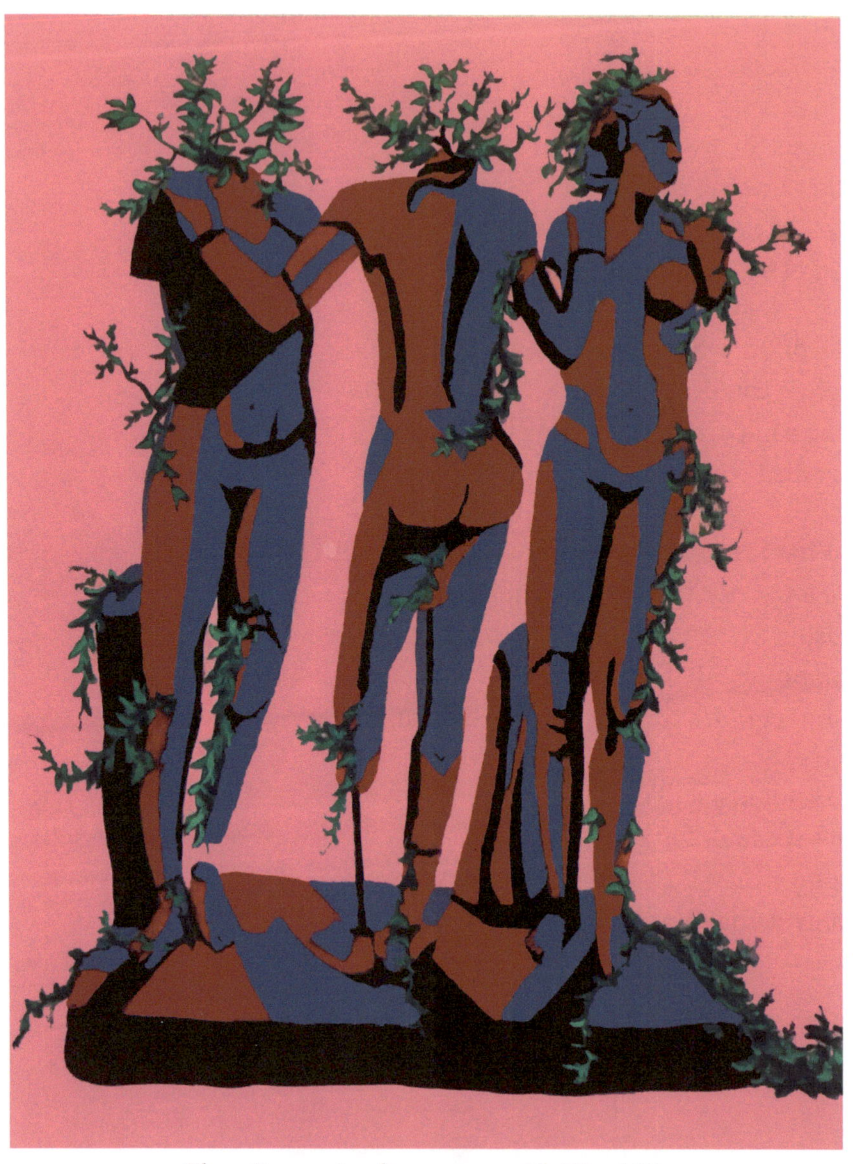

Three Graces. Acrylic on canvas, 16x20in, 2021.

Don't fall in love with an artist

She will carve your name into immortality,
penetrating through the viewer's gaze.
She'll leave impressionist marks of
your lips and your face
until that image becomes a blurry haze.

Did you know an artist feels deeply?
The cells in the body will replenish yearly,
but as soon as she hears the first letter
of her lover's name,
the dopamine rushes to her brain
for the beloved that she loved so dearly.

Don't fall in love with an artist.
For she'll be mesmerized by the birthmark on your right arm,
capturing every moment and writing you love letters.
She'll make your deepest insecurity feel like a lucky charm.

And I begged my heart not to fall in love with you
because I knew you wanted a fling and nothing more.
I craved him to explore the deepest parts of my soul,
yet he couldn't even make it past the shore.

But it's okay, though —
Even though what we had turned to dust,
we both found out what we wanted in a relationship.

It just wasn't us.

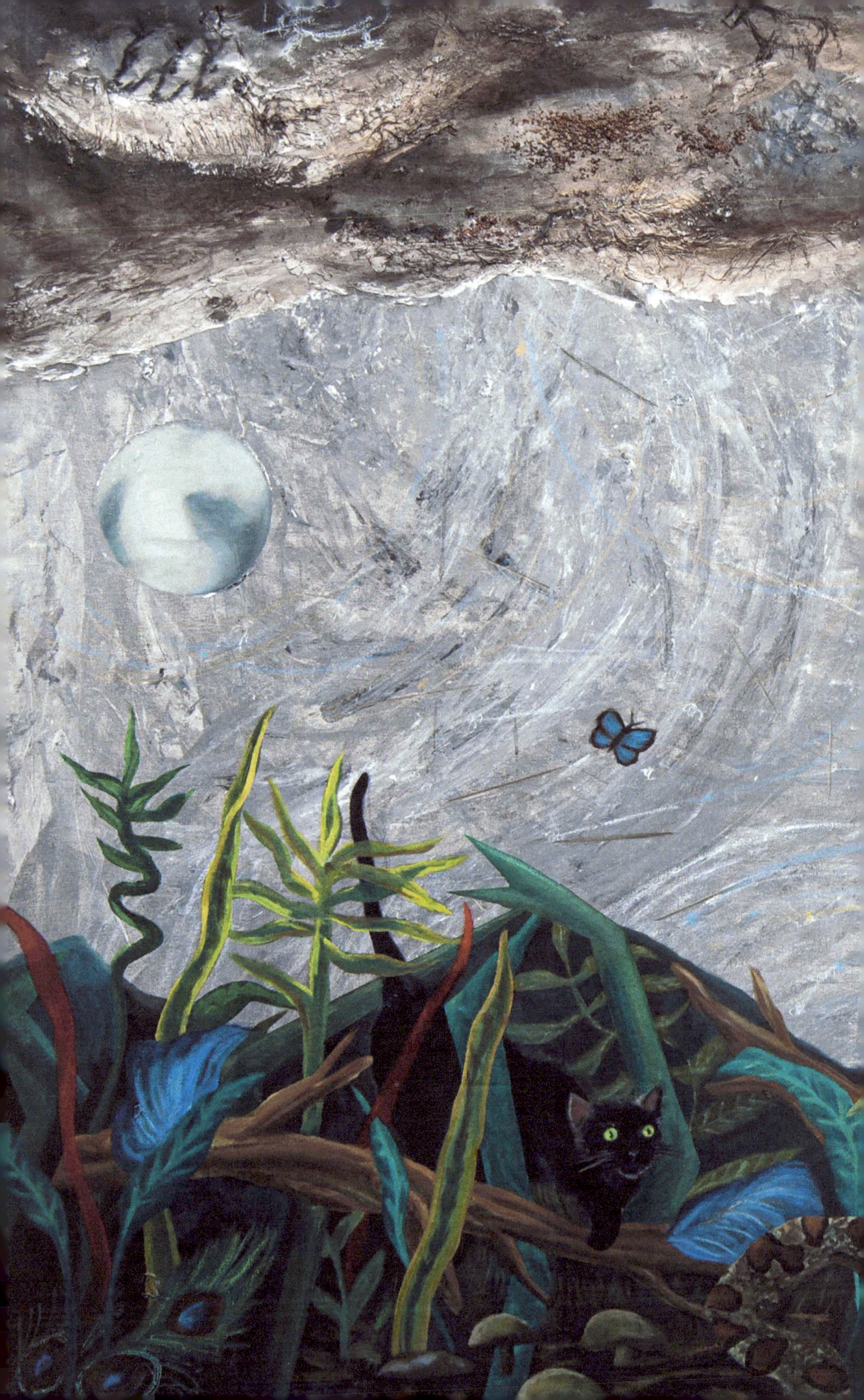

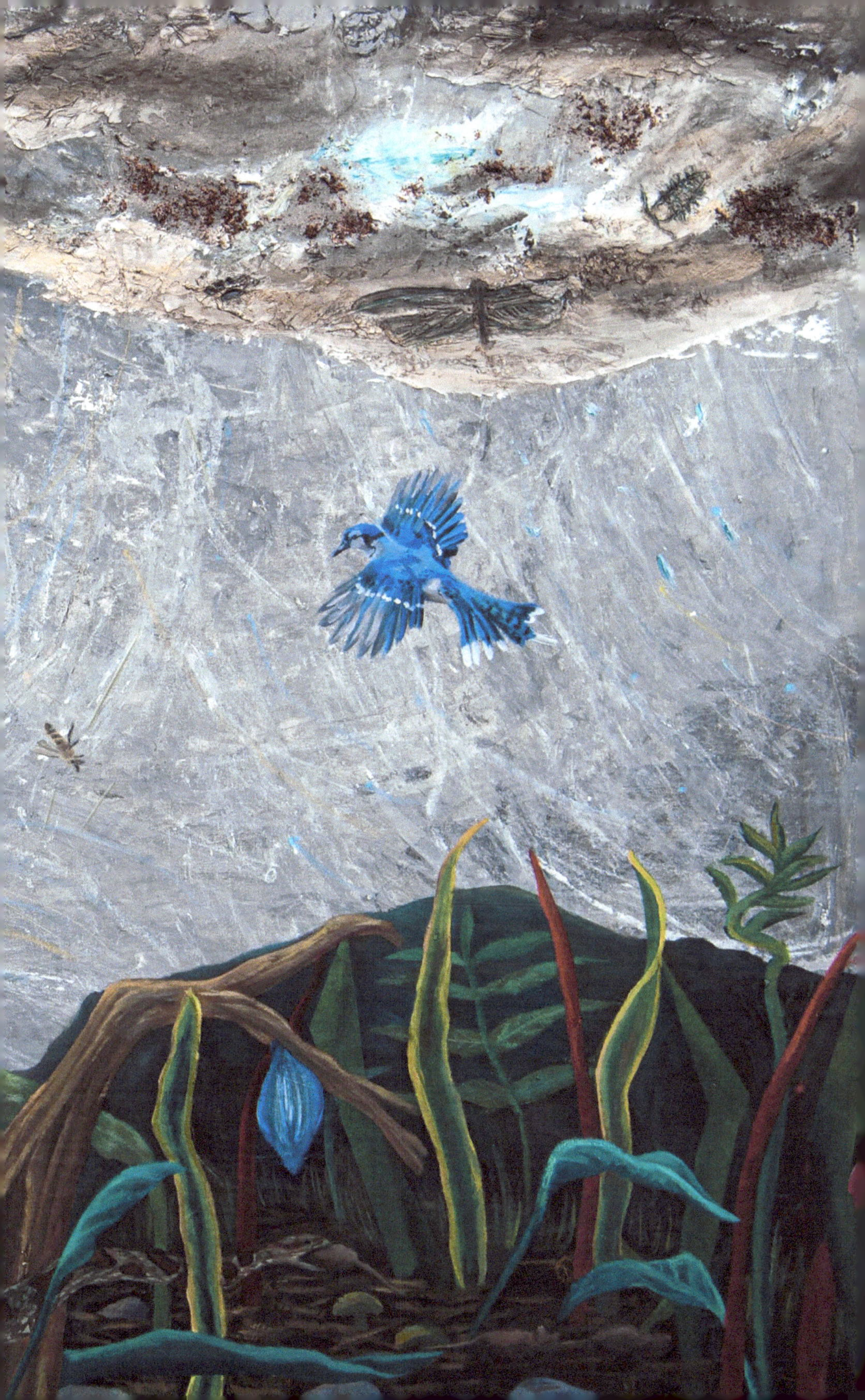

PART III

INTERCONNECTEDNESS WITH THE CYCLE OF LIFE & DREAMS

Growing up in a Catholic household, I was taught that there were only two paths after death: heaven or hell. However, life is rarely so clear-cut, especially in a world rich with diverse perspectives and resources. After losing someone dear to me, I felt compelled to explore alternative views on the afterlife. This journey led me through various texts and art forms, including Dante Alighieri's *Inferno*, cosmic theories, poetry, the *Egyptian Book of the Dead*, and Sogyal Rinpoche's *The Tibetan Book of Living and Dying*. I also engaged with spiritually charged artworks like Hilma af Klint's *The Paintings for the Temple* (1905-1915) and Hieronymus Bosch's *Garden of Earthly Delights* (1503-1515). These explorations have deeply influenced my approach to art, inspiring me to create mythical and spiritual realities. There is so much valuable information out there, but here are some things that I've learned:

- Decomposition and Rebirth: As our physical bodies decompose, our remains return to the earth and are reused. In essence, what is gone is never really gone but transformed in some particle or another. Reflecting the cyclical nature of existence.

- The Afterlife in Ancient Texts: In the guiding scroll of Anu's afterlife, the weighing of the heart against a feather symbolizes the purity of the soul. If Anu's heart is heavier, it is devoured by a crocodile; if lighter, he proceeds to meet Osiris, the king of the underworld.

- Dante's *Inferno*: Dante's 14th-century epic poem depicts his journey through the nine circles of hell, reflecting a timeless narrative where past and present converge in a vivid, eternal struggle. *Inferno* is followed by *Purgatorio* and *Paradiso* to describe the journey of the soul toward God. It was a dream Dante received that inspired him to write the story.

- Dreams: Existing in the space between consciousness and unconsciousness, much like the realm between life and death. Dreams can act as messengers, offering glimpses of the future, insights into our subconscious, connections to the collective unconscious, or revealing hidden symbolism. For instance, a dream involving a snake may reflect a personal desire for intimacy, while in ancient cultures, the snake often symbolized fertility and power. Ultimately, the interpretation of dreams should resonate with the dreamer, aligning with their unique experiences and beliefs.

- Living in the Moment: Embrace each moment as if it were your last. Cultivating a mindful presence is the practice of fully immersing yourself in the here and now, free from distractions. If you're eating, savor each bite. If you're walking, be with each step. While the future or afterlife remains uncertain, the present moment is all we truly have.

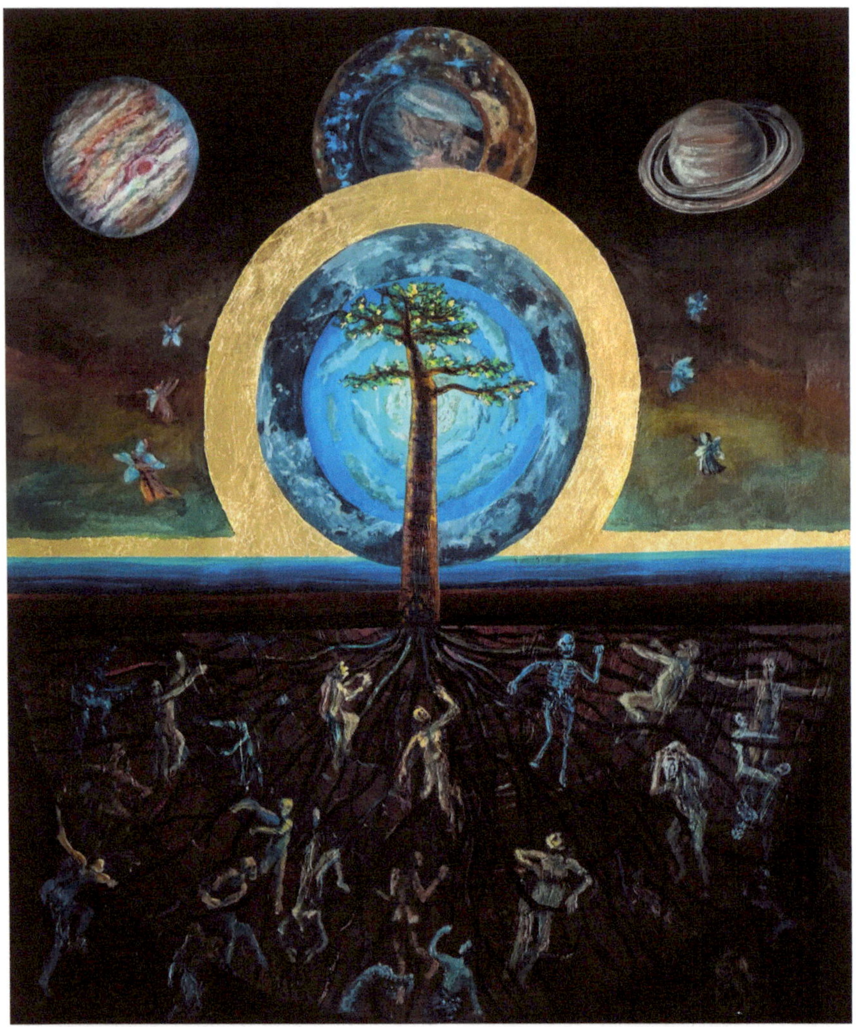

A Journey Between Two Dimensions, mixed media on canvas, 42"x32"in, 2022.

To confront one's mortality
gives a deep appreciation to
the impermanence of things —
being on the same coin
as the eternal in everything.

The afterlife drifts, whirls, and swirls;
bewilderment shifts, clarity opens the gate.
If one has lost touch with nature,
what then, is humanity's fate?

Everything is interconnected.
We don't live on the outside,
experiencing life from the other.
It's experienced on the inside,
a joyous river full of wonder.

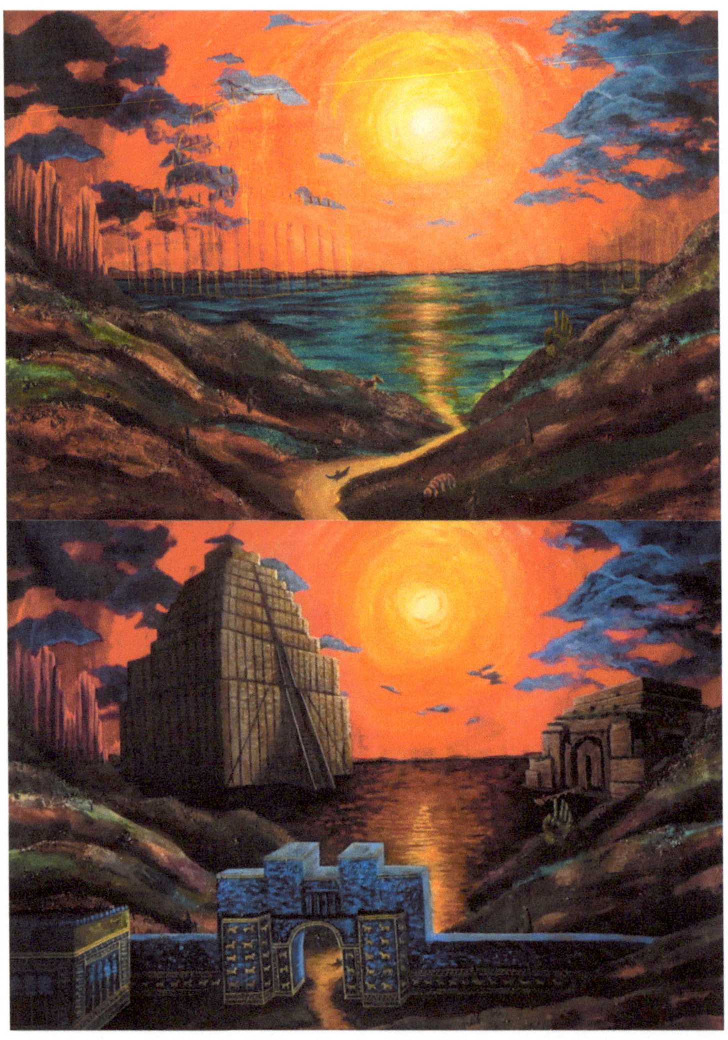

Into the Void. Mixed media on canvas, 65.2"x51"in, 2023 - 2024. A painting of Ancient Babylon depicts a lone boat traveling through the Ishtar Gate, past the Hanging Gardens of Babylon, and toward the Ziggurat. I've always been inspired by the story of humanity coming together to create a monumental structure, as told in the biblical tale of the Tower of Babel. According to Genesis 11:1-9, there was a time when all people on earth spoke the same language and united to build a city with a tower reaching the heavens. In response, the Lord created confusion by causing them to speak different languages, making it impossible for them to understand one another. This divine intervention led to the abandonment of the city and the scattering of its people across the world.

What was once there
sunken stories of Atlantis
deep beneath the ocean floor.

The high Tower of Babel
where humanity was once at peace,
now lies in ruins beyond distant shores.

The mind drifts away toward a new place,
not near the world we're in.
Tardigrades moving in different sizes,
a place born without sin.

No laws in a forgotten city
what is gone is never lost.
Knowledge from the past is still reused,
stories waiting to be crossed.

The microcosm meets the macrocosm,
meeting the dimension
called "reality."

Experiencing what is
a once-in-a-lifetime sanctity.

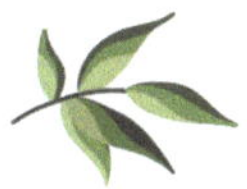

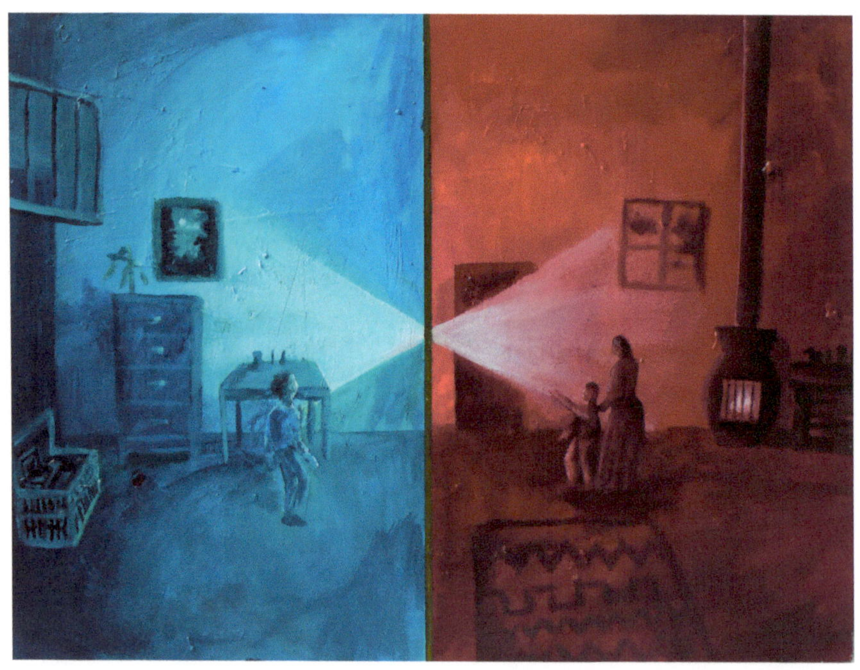

Dream of the Vivid Painting, mixed media on canvas, 18"x24"in, 2022.

The Dream of the Vivid Painting

October 18, 2022: In this dream, I was at a man's place — someone who felt familiar but whom I didn't quite recognize. As we talked, we examined various plants, and he was surprised that I knew which ones were poisonous. Our conversation continued as we went downstairs to the living room, where a mahogany drawer caught my eye.

Unexpectedly, a dark red beetle with black Egyptian hieroglyphs emerged from the mahogany drawer and moved toward a large gold Egyptian treasure chest. The chest kept opening to reveal more boxes inside, like Russian Matryoshka dolls, each one smaller than the last. Eventually, the bug crawled into the smallest chest. When I turned back toward the man, he showed me a painting and asked, "What do you feel when you see this painting?" I reflected on how it felt like time traveling, magical, and connected to alchemy. When I woke up, I painted the painting that I saw in the dream.

I later asked several people what they felt about the painting, and their interpretations aligned with mine—it seemed like a portal related to time travel. What struck me was how vivid the dream was; I could see the painting's blue and red hues, the characters and objects depicted, and the light shining through the center. As I continued to work on depicting dreams during my thesis semester, the more vivid my dreams became. Each person interprets the dream's meaning differently, but to me, it felt like someone communicating across space and time. A friend suggested that the man on the left might be trying to communicate with his younger self on the right. In the end, there is no wrong answer.

PART IV

INTERCONNECTEDNESS. EMPTINESS.

At this point, I'm embracing my imperfections and loving who I am in this physical human body, made from stardust and covered in skin. Each bump and curve reflects the divine and I see this beauty in everything and everyone I encounter — I wonder if they see it too. We are all humans at the end of the day. "Seeing emptiness, have compassion" - Milarepa.

The universe has been expanding since the Big Bang and remains present around us today. Everything is in constant flux. As Ferguson writes, "The conception of the universe as an interconnected web of connections is one of two major themes that reoccur throughout modern physics. The other theme is the realization that the cosmic web is intrinsically dynamic." This idea of continuation is evident in our DNA from our ancestors that are no longer alive in their bodies, but they continue to exist in ours. Each cell carries a sacred bundle of genetic material passed down through thousands of generations. Humanity has left its mark on the world—from cave drawings to civilizations, art, and stories. There is a universal emotion or storytelling that connects us to our ancestors. It's time we reconnect with that source of creativity.

As our ancestors honored the land, we also need to reconnect and honour Earth. Whether it's upcycling materials, picking up litter, or planting a seed, every small gesture counts toward creating a better place to be in for centuries to come.

Just as a single stone creates ripples across a pond, each of our actions and thoughts sends out waves of change.

The universe is vast, and the probability of being here on Earth is said to be a rare 1 in 400 trillion. We are stardust creatures with the consciousness to do what is right: to love, to feel the grass once more, and to remember what it's like to be alive.

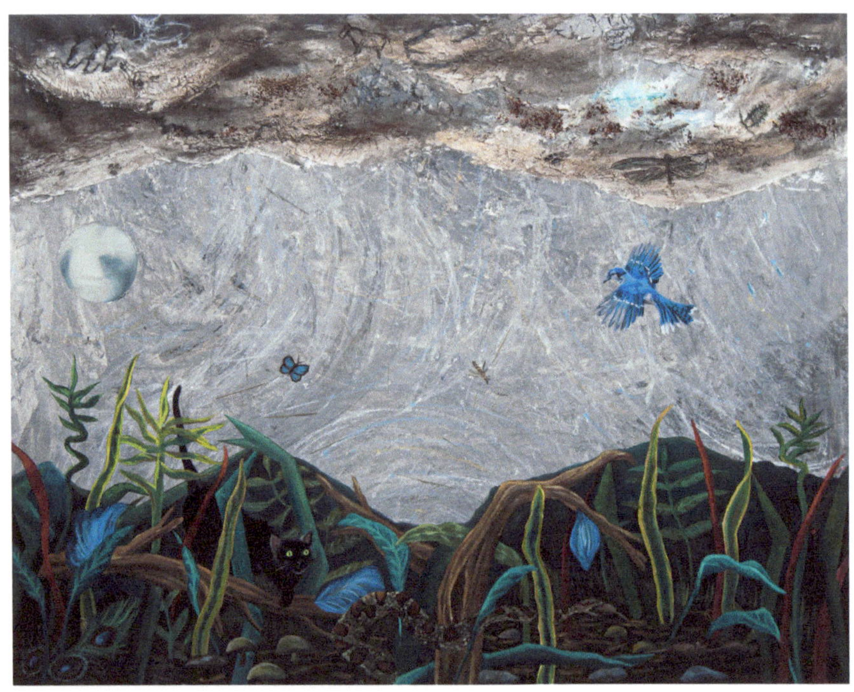

After the Big Bang. Acrylic paint, oil paint, oil pastel, modeling paste, harvested walnut shell on canvas, 52"x65"in, 2023. Traces of Buwan's paw prints are seen on the top part of the painting, as well as sketches and fossils to imitate those found in Chauvet Cave 32,000 years ago. Gestural marks of the Big Bang explosion cover the midground with all its particles floating through space, while traces of the past are mixed in with the present to show that what is gone is never lost. The particles from the Big Bang are still present around us today and remain in constant flux in the great dance of the cycle of life.

Filling An Empty Cup

Sometimes I feel as light as a pencil
or the opaqueness of oil.
My hand gestures with the wind,
and my feet dig into the soil.

I'm grounded by the bird song
filling the soundless blue sky.
Then contemplate the velocity
of the bees that pass by.

My cup becomes empty, away
from worries, desires, words, and memory.
What's the use of filling a cup with
neither positive nor negative energy?

Empty. No expectations, no future,
or past, nor this, or that.
In a world of obscurity, who's to say
what's fiction or what's fact?

We're one out of a billion stars,
planets, and galaxies across the skies.
One rule here is not the same
definite rule that applies.

Fantasy and reality
lost between the two.
When this world seems dream-like,
it creates something new.

Full of different universes
millions of atoms in the sand.
We hold the wanders of the stars
in the palm of our hand.

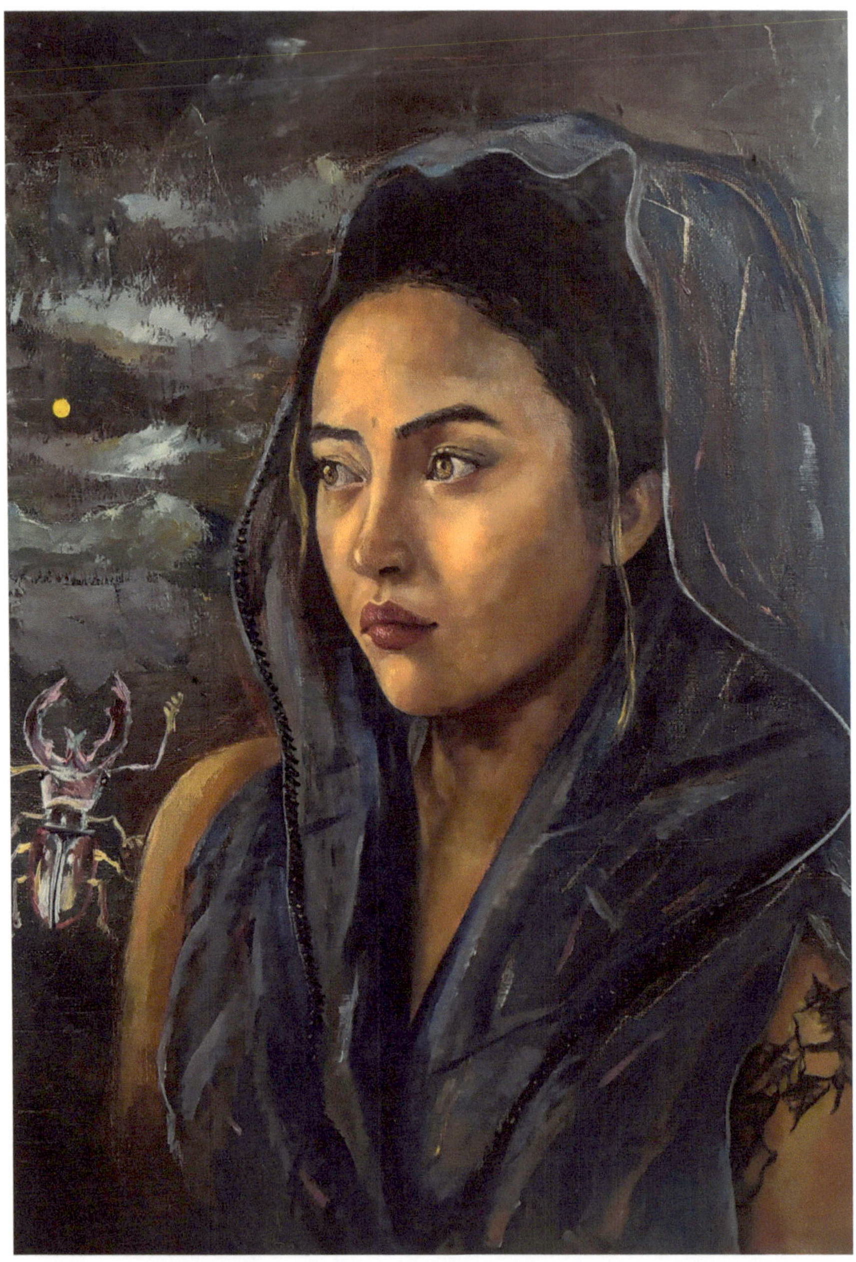

The Veiled one. Mixed media on canvas, 18"x16"in, 2024.

Emptiness

A piece of advice from a businessman was to have a word that
describes what it is you want to be and describes who you are.
My word was emptiness.

I keep trying to rush,
rush my ideas, my process, my future,
it leaves me anxious and worried
that what I've done is not enough.

I want to empty myself each day because each day is new.
Because it's worth it when there's no expectation.
Because why want more when I have enough?
Because I'm a work in progress.

Because I can't have all the answers.
Because silence brings answers from the universe.
Because we're accustomed to being who we are.
Because we can never be set in our ways.

Because I deserve to be empty of worry.
Because "I" is disguised as ego.
Because who is "I" but not a construct?
Because it puts happy and sad away.

Because I can focus on now.
The why for art, why I do it, is related to it.
I become so empty but my mind is full of ideas.

Ideas worth sharing with the world,
worth harmonizing as messages from above,
as a sign of knowingness and
a sign of being at peace with the present.

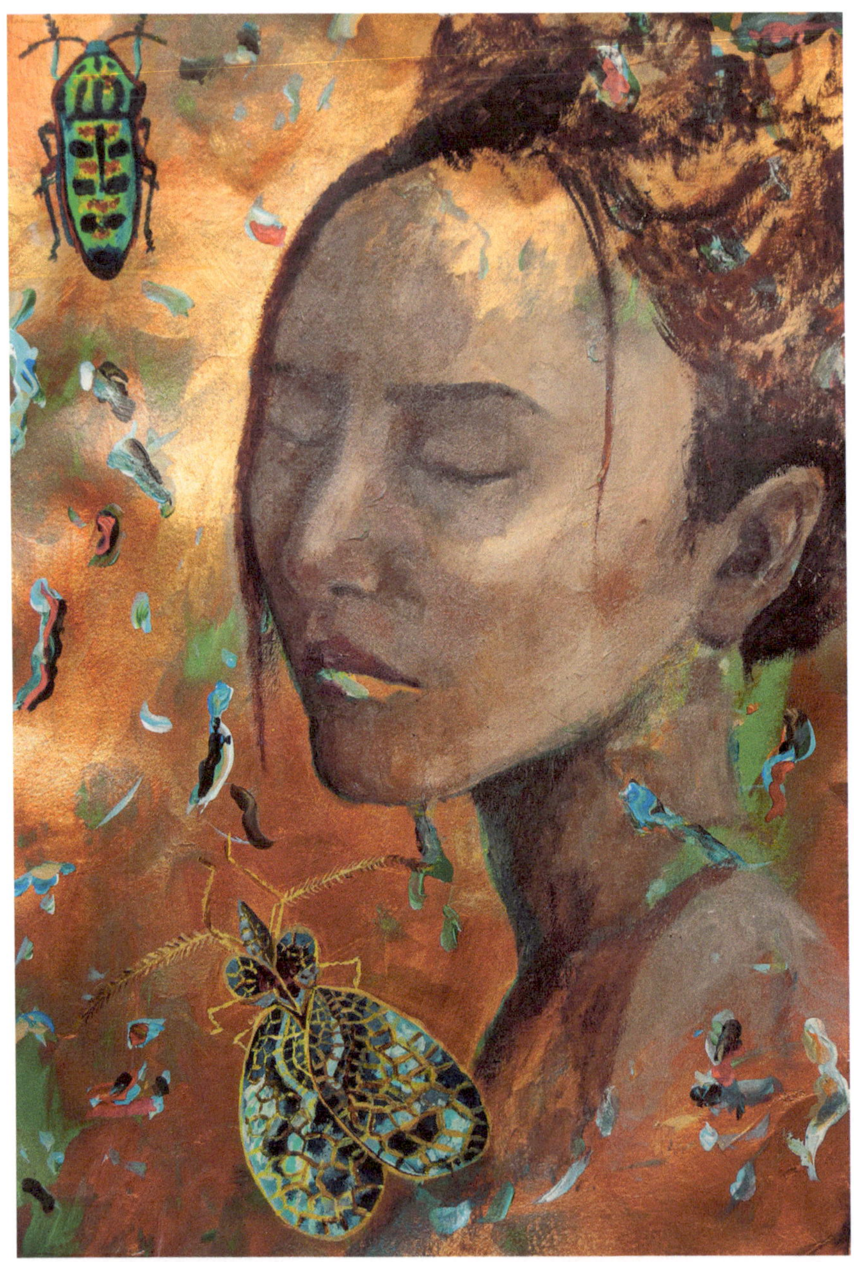

Contemplation. Mixed media on paper, 8"x10"in, 2023.

Being Content

I've seen people happy
with the little they have,
or underwhelmed with all
the riches imaginable.

Once we make happiness
an external thing,
it can never be fulfilled —
for that, is also perishable.

If we aren't content
with what we have now,
then having more or better
will not make the soul sing.

Want nothing, be empty.
There is an ocean
inside your heart
that only emptiness brings.

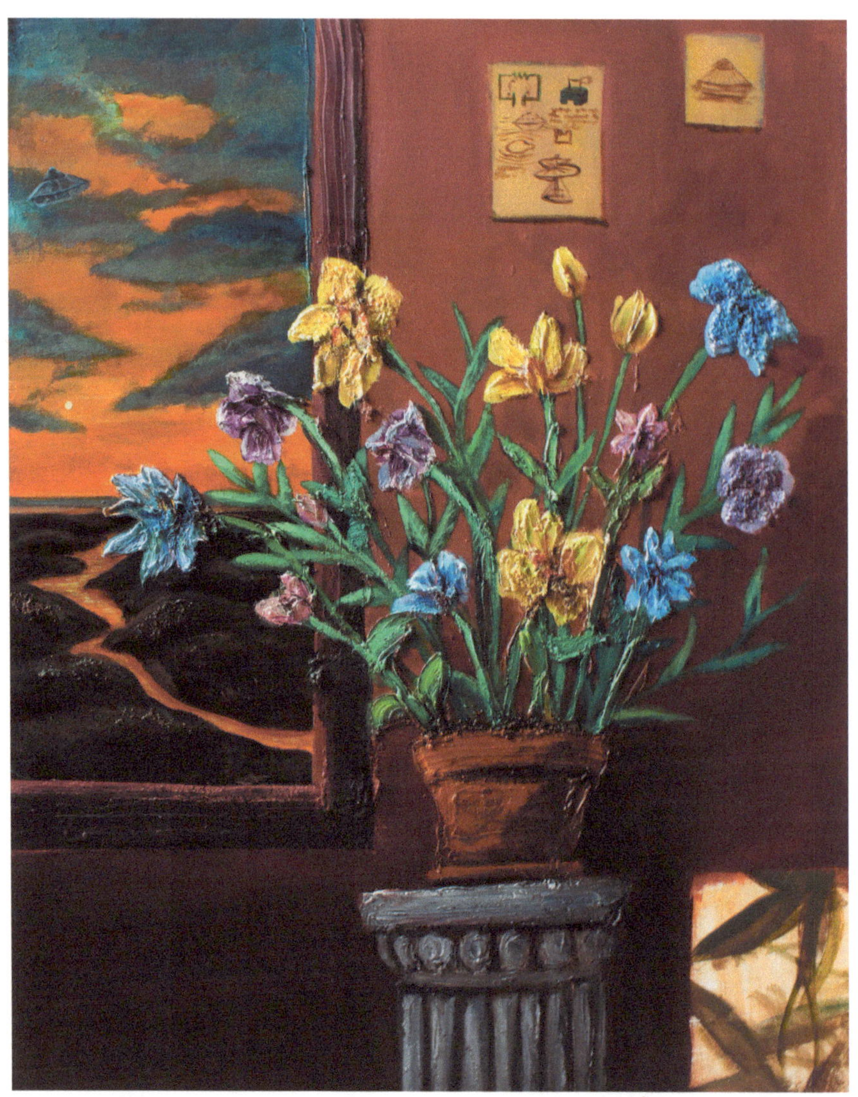

Flowers With Notes. Mixed media on canvas, 24"x30"in, 2022.

There are days when
I move more slowly.
As if playing the piano,
searching for the right key

No rush with a body
that wants to rest,
getting lost in silence
is the ultimate test.

There's no urgency to push,
or climb the social ladder.
Being stuck in a rat race
makes the heart shatter.

My mind needs medicine
it heals from nature's sound,
in each exhale that flows
it's silent, yet profound.

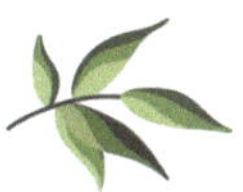

Connecting With Self

How beautiful is the human body,
capable of so many things.
We get so caught up in routine,
every notification and ring.

To appreciate this, right now,
is all that we can do.
What better way to honor this beingness
than to fully connect with you.

I am but an instrument
for the divine to express ideas.
This mouth, this face, these hands —
all a mere reflection of the creator's designs.

Love has no confines

When was the last time
you loved without expectation?
We believe it's this cozy feeling,
a happy one with instant gratification.

Why is it that when we think of love,
something or someone comes to mind?
When will you find it in the moment,
within the present state of mind?

I see love as this —
this creation, this breathing, this spirit kept alive.
The mysteries of your being,
and the secrets you keep inside.

Don't wait to fall in love —
do it now in this moment,
as you breathe in, take in love.

Because love isn't a moment or a person,
It's a state of being,
a divine message
carried on the wings of a dove.

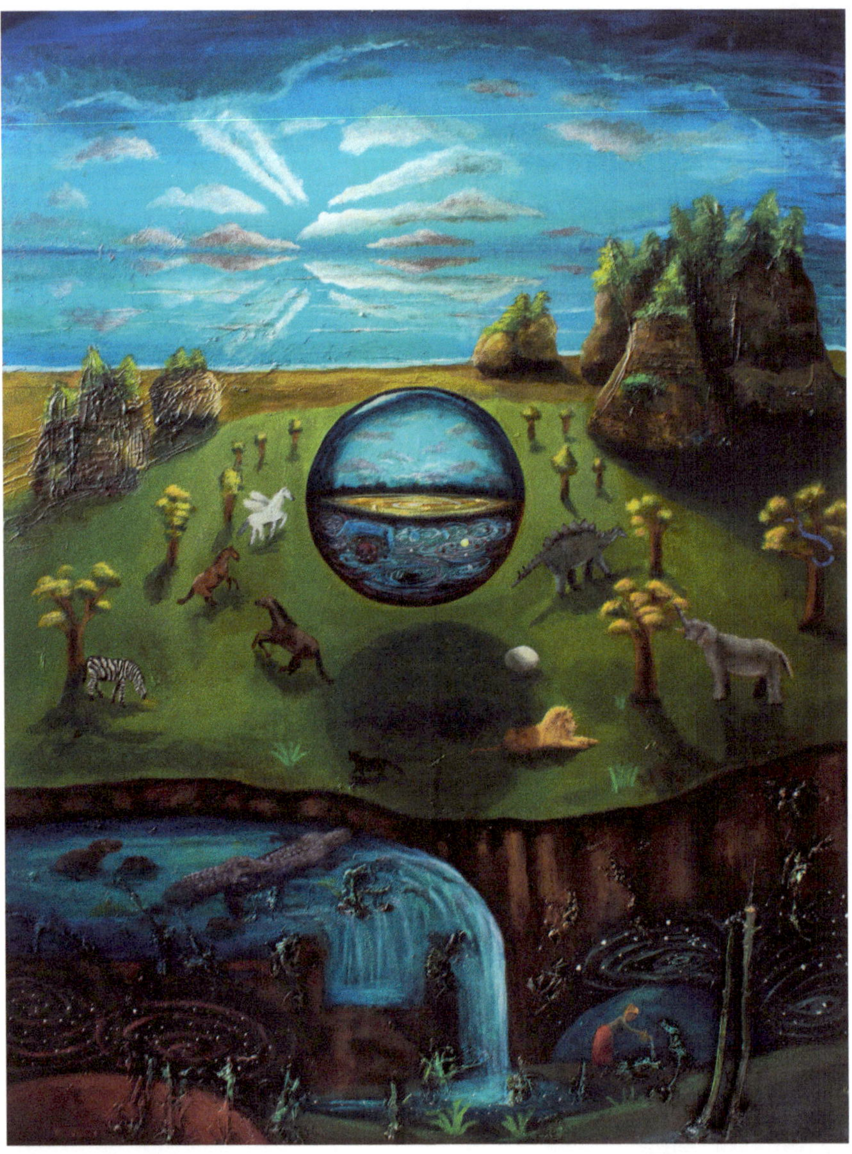

Primordial Soup. Acrylic paint, oil paint, branches, plants, modeling paste, gloss varnish on canvas, 30"x40"in, 2023 Primordial Soup imagines creation of how life came to be, starting from the early Earth's oceans filled with organic molecules. The painting has a circle in the center with a yellow area representing the microcosm of cells clashing together to form creation. At the same time, the circle also symbolizes the macrocosm of the universe by showing the vastness of the painting and the complexity of creation.

Universe Collapsing in Itself

Soon the universe will collapse
it has no permanence being here.
Out of the joyful being of creation,
there will be nothing left near.

Where does consciousness go then,
if there are no more traces of being?
A shout to the void,
with no eyes left seeing.

It may be billions of years
before the time is yet to come.
Yet I'll remember you, friend,
in a faraway place where you're from,

Your beingness is eternal,
stardust, minerals, and more.
Yet you confine yourself to a prison,
with negative thoughts to endure.

Rarity of one in 400 trillion,
take this chance and do it right.
The outside skin conceals your inner radiance,
scintillating as the sun's light.

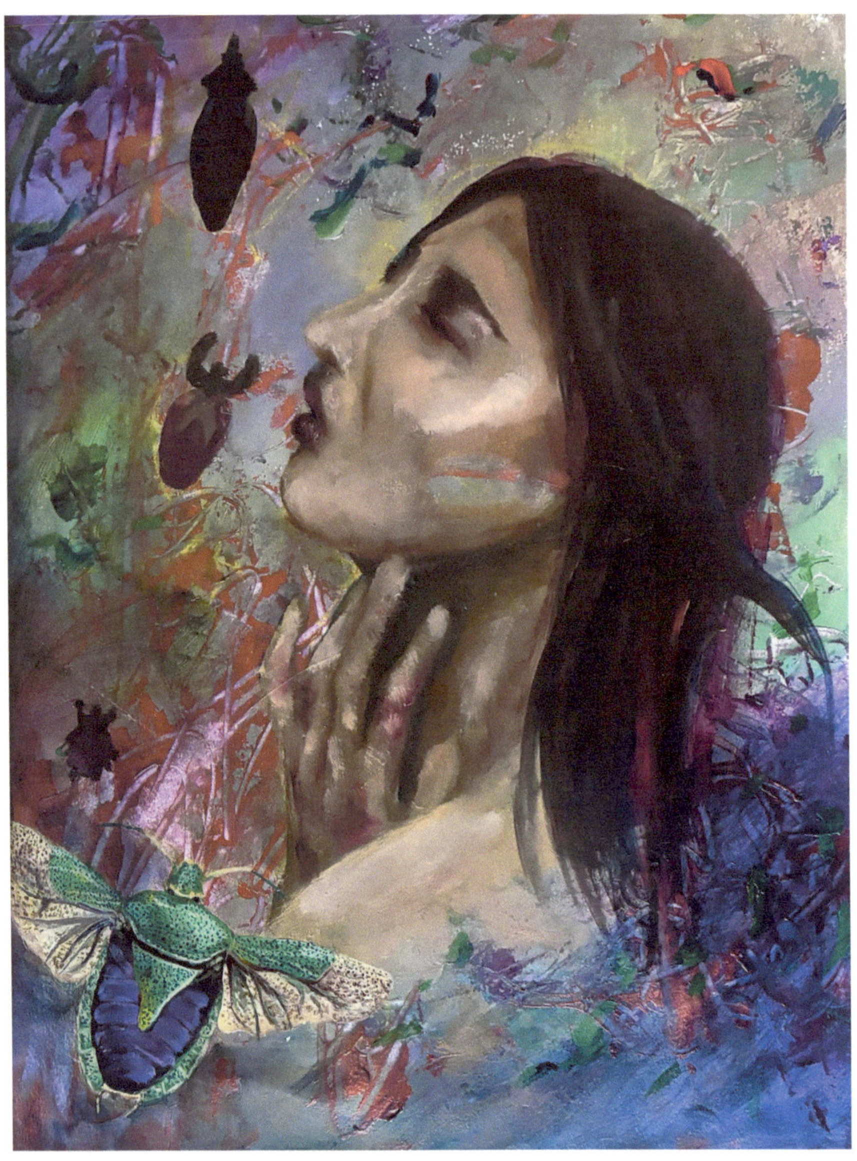

Surrender, mixed media on paper, 12"x16"in, 2024.

If it's not the love
that turns the bitterness sweet
or the type of love capable to
sweep me off my feet.

If it's not the type of love
that makes the worries disappear,
or erases one's sorrows,
and dissipates all fear.

It's the only love given by the One
who knows all.
Inside the believer
is true love's call.

Buried in the musk and frankincense,
love's fragrance leaves its traces.
Now it's found everywhere in
All the trees, plants, and faces.

PART V.

THE HEALING JOURNEY.

Journeying to the deepest parts of the psyche can be both difficult yet rewarding. Some parts you think you've healed from may sneak up on you like a garden snake slithering through a field of tall grass. Remember that healing is an ongoing process. There are unexpected moments when I find myself grieving over my brother, cherishing the memories we shared. Healing doesn't mean achieving perfection; it's learning to be strong despite what we've gone through. Who you are is not set on stone, so keep reshaping yourself until you find satisfaction. Here are some practices that have guided me on my path to healing:

- Singing, dancing, and listening to music, embracing the freedom of self-expression.

- Finding a way to release negative emotions can make you feel better afterward. For me, it's creating art or sharing my feelings with someone. Others might create music, go to therapy, or engage in physical activity. Find what feels right for you, ensuring that you don't hurt others along the way.

- Painting in my authentic state – naked – discovering liberation in vulnerability.

- Positive affirmations. Even if you don't believe it, keep on repeating it until you do. Words hold power, and your body responds to them. Keep nurturing yourself with positivity.

- Immersing myself in reading books that I find interesting and learning about new topics.

- Creating collages from magazines, sketches, and notebooks as a form of artistic exploration.

- Writing poetry or journaling to express and process emotions.

- Traveling: Whether it's exploring a new country, city, or simply taking a different route home, travel can be refreshing. A fresh perspective opens the mind to new ideas.

- Solo dates: Treat yourself to a date occasionally. It's a great way to nurture self-love.

- Mindfulness and meditation: Regular practice helps cultivate inner peace and greater self-awareness.

- Having a yoga or exercise practice. Tell yourself that you will do it for 5 minutes. Sometimes that 5 minutes turns into 1 hour. A healthy body is a healthy mind.

- Walking in nature to ground myself or get fresh air. I once read that the number of trees you see per day can increase your happiness.

- Experimenting with new recipes even though it doesn't come out the way I want.

- Being mindful of self-talk: When I catch myself in a negative or habitual thought pattern, I focus on shifting toward a positive inner dialogue. This is where positive affirmations play a key role.

- Cultivating self-awareness by observing my breath: whether shallow, rapid, mindful, or slow and steady. Calm, deep, steady breaths help calm the mind during stressful situations.

- Pushing myself outside my comfort zone to embrace growth and new experiences.

- Gratitude list: listing 3 things that you're grateful for each day will shift the mindset from wanting more to being happy with what you currently have.

- Embrace the moment: You're incredibly fortunate to be exactly where you are right now. Savor each second, and don't let doubt steal away the present. You are more than enough.

- Practice patience and self-compassion: be your own best friend because at the end, it's you who sits through the thoughts.

CONCLUSION.

"Yesterday I was clever, so I wanted to change the world.
Today I am wise, so I am changing myself." – Rumi.

What began as a journey of healing from heartbreak and loss has transformed into a deeper understanding of love—love for others, for our environment, and for the world. Though life can be challenging, approaching it with love nurtures not only ourselves but future generations.

When I first started writing, I was in a place of pain. My healing had to come first before I could take the next step. As I healed, I opened my heart to help others on similar journeys. By healing ourselves, we break cycles of trauma, ensuring they aren't passed on. Trauma is not only emotional or mental—it's reflected in our actions and how they shape the world around us.

Imagine a caregiver who nurtures your core being, offering unconditional love and striving to make the world a better place for you. Some of us may not have had that figure, and I didn't either, but I'm learning to become that person for myself. The actions we take today will shape future generations, our society, and the environment.

Change starts within. Begin small, build momentum, and one day you'll look back and see how far you've come. You are capable of so much more than you realize. Heal, grow, create, and tap into your full potential. Be the change you wish to see. Repeat.

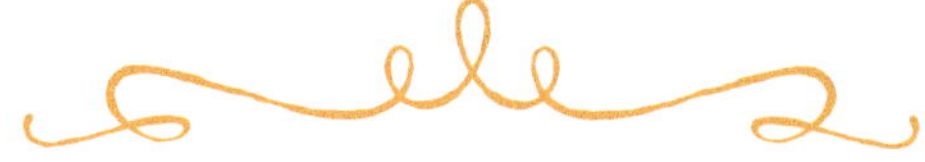

BIBLIOGRAPHY

Alighieri, Dante. *The Divine Comedy of Dante Alighieri: Inferno, Purgatory, Paradise* 1265-1321. New York: The Union Library Association, 1935.

Apostol, M., Virgil. *Way of the Ancient Healer. Sacred teachings from the Philippine Ancestral Traditions.* Berkeley, California, 2010.

Ferguson, E. "Einstein, Sacred Science, And Quantum Leaps A Comparative Analysis Of Western Science, Native Science And Quantum Physics Paradigm." 2005. Pp. 50-73.

Herzog, Werner, director. *Cave of Forgotten Dreams.* 2011.

Kamrin, Janice. "Scrolling through Imhotep's Book of the Dead." Metmuseum.org, 12 July 2016, https://www.metmuseum.org/blogs/now-at-the-met/2016/book-of-the-dead.

Rysdyk, Evelyn. *Shamanic Creativity: Free the Imagination with Rituals, Energy Work, and Spirit Journeying.* Destiny Books. 2022.

Tzu, Lao. *Tao Te Ching,* translated by J.H McDonald. 1996.

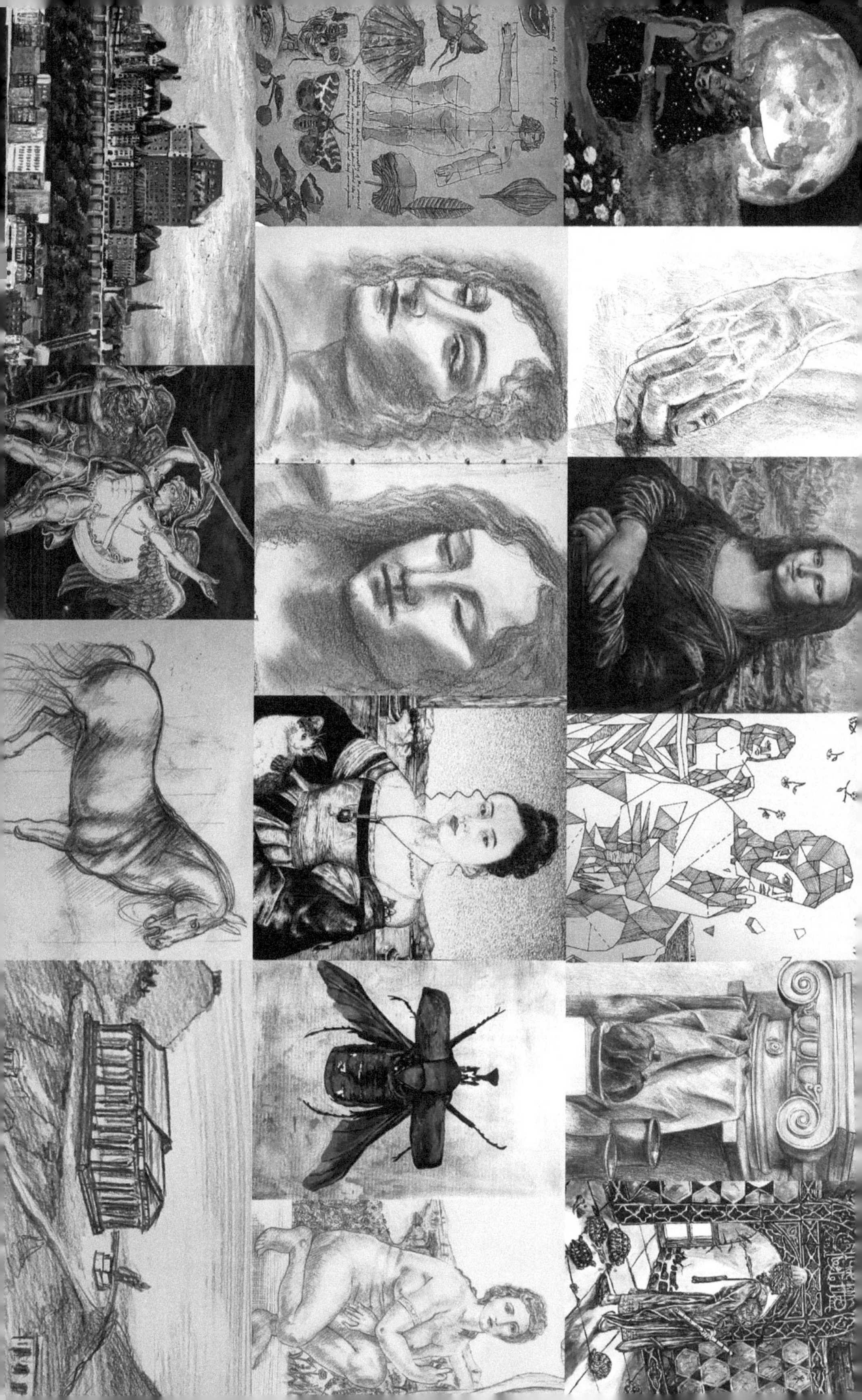